"Seeing what God has done in someone else's life can be just the inspiration you need. These courageous stories of girls set apart in character, passion, and destiny will call out the Esther in you, for such a time as this. Way to lead the charge, Lisa!"

NICOLE C. MULLEN, FOUR-TIME DOVE AWARD–WINNING
SINGER/SONGWRITER

"This fantastic book reminded me that my destiny is not determined by my appearance, fashion know-how, or circle of friends. My worth is found only in the purpose-filled identity of Christ's unfathomable love."

JOY WILLIAMS, THREE-TIME DOVE AWARD NOMINEE,
BEST NEW ARTIST, CCM READERS' AWARDS 2002

"I love this book! It's never too early or too late to be a part of Generation Esther. It only takes one to change a nation, and that one could be you. Read this book and you will be charged with Esther-sized girl power!"

NATALIE GRANT, SINGER/SONGWRITER

"Lisa Ryan has filled these pages with young women who have answered God's call with a heartfelt yes—even when it has cost them! Girls, you will be pumped with the courage and the desire to do the same. Be part of Gen-E! Be God's girl and rock your generation for Jesus!"

ANDREA STEPHENS, BRIO beauty editor,
AUTHOR OF STUFF A GIRL'S GOTTA KNOW

"Generation Esther is full of inspiring stories of triumph and grace. God has a great destiny for those who are willing to be used by Him. Another home run, Lisa!"

LISA KIMMEY, OUT OF EDEN

generation esther

lisa ryan

Multnomah® Publishers *Sisters, Oregon*

GENERATION ESTHER
published by Multnomah Publishers, Inc.

© 2003 by Lisa Ryan
International Standard Book Number: 1-59052-194-3

Cover design by Steve Gardner
Cover images by Corbis

Unless otherwise indicated, Scripture quotations are from:
The Holy Bible, New International Version
© 1973, 1984 by International Bible Society,
used by permission of Zondervan Publishing House
Other Scripture quotations are from:
The Holy Bible, New King James Version (NKJV)
© 1984 by Thomas Nelson, Inc.
The Message by Eugene H. Peterson, Copyright © 1993, 1994, 1995, 1996, 2000.
Used by permission of NavPress Publishing Group. All rights reserved.
Holy Bible, New Living Translation (NLT)
© 1996. Used by permission of Tyndale House Publishers, Inc.
All rights reserved.

For information:
MULTNOMAH PUBLISHERS, INC.
POST OFFICE BOX 1720
SISTERS, OREGON 97759

Library of Congress Cataloging-in-Publication Data

Ryan, Lisa.
   Generation Esther / by Lisa Ryan.
      p. cm.
Includes bibliographical references (p.157).
   ISBN 1-59052-194-3
   1. Girls—Religious life. 2. Girls—Conduct of life. 3. Esther, Queen of Persia. I. Title.
   BV4551.3.R93 2003
   248.8'43—dc21

                                        2003012406

03 04 05 06 07 08—10 9 8 7 6 5 4 3 2 1 0

This book is dedicated to all the girls who
are answering the call to join
God's Girl Movement and are:
rising up to live set-apart lives,
making godly choices,
walking in character,
facing challenges,
and stepping out in courage…
for such a time as this.
You are my heroes, and this is for you—Generation Esther.

Contents

Gratitude

My humble and heart-gushing thanks to:

My Lord, for allowing me to be a steward of this message to young women. You have been so faithful to divinely cross my path with some of Your modern-day Esthers, and I am honored and privileged to share their stories.

My family, who continually encouraged me month after month. To my husband, Marcus, for always believing in me, for postponing his dissertation at times so I could monopolize the computer, for his expert skill in editing, and for constantly fixing the computer when his technically challenged wife messed it up. To my daughters, Quinlyn, Logan, and Madelin, for their daily prayer for "Mommy to finish her book."

My circle of maiden friends, who continue to advise, inspire, challenge, and cheer me on: Marti, Kim, Paula, Maria, Karen, and Darlene. I love you ladies.

Renee DeLoriea, for laying the foundation and her gift of encouragement.

Jim Lund, for saving the day and getting the girl thing.

Jennifer Gott, for finding my voice and the voice of this generation.

My publishing family at Multnomah—it takes a team of people to take a book from an idea to the reader's hands. Without this team, *Generation Esther* would still be just an idea. I thank them for believing in me and believing in you.

Generation Esther

lisaryan

D o you believe what most TV shows, movies, songs, magazines, Internet sites, and romance novels are telling you about girl power? That a girl's worth and power come from showing skin and curves to get a guy's attention, flirting up a storm, teasing like a pop-starlet, or sleeping around? Or that happiness can be found only by being the prettiest, best-dressed, snobbiest Queen Bee of them all? Maybe you've been dipping your toe in the water or even jumping in on the action because you think all the other girls are doing it. Could it really be that all the other girls are grabbing their chance to prove they're the kind of sexual bait no man can resist? That they're all clawing their way to the top of the most-popular-girl food chain, and you may as well join them?

Well, I have news for you: Not all girls are doing that! And not all girls act that way! In fact, a lot of girls are choosing an entirely different approach to life altogether. They're rebelling against the destructive messages of this world and forging their own purposeful path—you could even call them *countercultural*.

Fewer and fewer girls today are buying into the idea that making others drool or knowing how to "work it" is a sign that a girl has it together. Instead of being all about themselves, they're helping others. Instead of stabbing others in the back, they're protecting their sisters. They're thinking a whole lot more about who they are instead of about how much they can get. Basically, they're throwing off the junk that makes a girl weak and putting on the stuff that makes a girl strong— really strong—because she's empowered by God!

I call the teenage girls and young women who are part of this fresh move of God "Generation Esther." These young women (instead of Gen-X or Gen-Y, you could call them *Gen-E*) aren't buying the bill of goods that's being sold to the rest of today's generation. They have a deep hunger for real and personal spiritual experiences and for having a purpose worth living for—and even dying for.

Generation Esther girls aren't settling for the dark spiritual experiences promoted by the huge number of TV programs and movies that invite curious young women to experiment with witchcraft. They're also not reaching into the bag of tricks being offered by reality TV shows (and how "real" are those shows anyway? C'mon!), which often advocate guy hopping and backstabbing. They're not settling for what might make them feel good for the moment, but will wound them in the end. And they're certainly not allowing themselves to be used to fill the wallets of an industry that pumps out messages inviting them to hate their parents (or worse), disrespect authority, embrace apathy, party their brains out, live for sex, or commit suicide.

The terrorism acts of 9/11 have become a defining event for this generation. After 9/11, people suddenly became more serious about their lives and started trying to figure out how to make them really count. This trend is especially visible among young people. I have seen it firsthand among the hundreds of young women who have e-mailed me—from both the U.S. and many countries around the world—to tell me that they are radically sold out to living a life that is set apart for God.

I began receiving these e-mails when my first book, *For Such a Time as This,* was released in the summer of 2001. After reading the book (which is based on the story of Esther in the Bible), one by one, girls shared with me how the example of Esther's life is playing out in their own lives. Whether they are in a time of preparation, right smack in the middle of a crisis, or making courageous choices, they are identifying with Esther and recognizing how God is taking them through many of the same steps He took Esther through. Even in the midst of great challenges to their faith and character, these modern-day Esthers are rising to the call.

WHY ESTHER?

I have always loved the story of Esther, and her example is still relevant to young women—perhaps now more than ever. This OT (Old Testament, that is) teenager was more than just a pretty face. She faced challenges, made difficult choices, handled crises, and answered God's call on her life. Because of her obedience, courage, and wisdom, people's lives were saved and God's purpose in a nation was accomplished.

And God is *still* looking for young women of character and courage to accomplish His purposes. He is looking for average teenage girls and young women *like you,* who will return to timeless character values such as virtue, purity, obedience, courage, kindness, wisdom, and devotion. Right now, God is preparing and using many young women to make such a difference in the world that they will be part of shaping history.

Each generation before yours has had its "Esthers"—those young women who had the kind of character qualities that made it possible for God to use them in remarkable ways to fulfill His plans. Today, God is calling Generation Esther and building on the foundation of previous generations. But this larger collective move of God is also being lived out in the lives of individual girls like you.

Now is the time to step into the role you are destined to play in God's eternal plan.

Is God calling you to join Generation Esther? Are you feeling convicted, or impressed upon by God, to become set apart for a purpose that is bigger than you?

To help you recognize some of the ways God shapes and raises up average girls like you to be modern-day Esthers, we'll first look back at the life of the biblical role model, Esther. Then, as we look at the lives of some modern-day Esthers and see how they are rising to the call, you'll be able to identify the Esther in you...*for such a time as this.*

chapter one

For Such a Time as This

queenesther

sther's story is a legendary tale of an ordinary girl being used by God in an extraordinary way. It's the story of a young orphan girl from a common background who was suddenly thrust into a beauty contest and quickly elevated to the role of queen of a vast kingdom (kind of a Cinderella story, really). But this teenage girl hid a secret that could have killed her. Then a turn of events forced her to decide whether or not she would lay her life on the line to protect her people from destruction. Only *she* could save them.

Sounds like a script for a Hollywood movie, doesn't it? But this story is true.

Even if you've already read the story of Esther in the Bible or my first book, *For Such a Time as This,* I think you'll want to dig a little deeper with me into Esther's life. Why? Because comparing the life of this timeless role model with the lives of young women today who exhibit similar characteristics will help you better understand the ways God is working in *your* life. We'll look at:

- what it is about Esther that has made her a role model for generations to come.
- the ways Esther expressed her character that positioned her for this noble task.
- the critical choices Esther made that set her apart from others.
- the courage it took to be God's girl in a moment of crisis.

Choices…challenges…a crisis…and a call—Esther faced them all. But guess what? So will you. And how you respond to these situations will determine how God uses you in your generation.

To discover how Esther's example can be applied in our lives today, let's take a look at her story—and how God shaped an ordinary life into an extraordinary one.

A YOUNG GIRL IS CHOSEN
FOR A MAN-SIZED TASK

Esther was a girl who…

Hold up. Stop right there! A girl?

Before we go any further, let's make sure we get something that might be easy to skim right over. *Esther was a girl.* It's pretty amazing and encouraging that right before a crisis for His people was about to unfold, God put His confidence in an average teenage girl. Of all the people God could have chosen to protect the Jews when they were being threatened with annihilation, He chose a girl! That tells us right away that God delights in His girls and wants to use them to touch His world in uniquely feminine ways. It seems that sometimes, the best guy for the job is a girl! Both then and now, His Holy Spirit is the *only* source of bona fide "girl power."

Esther didn't just wake up one day, look at her Palm Pilot, realize it was her date with destiny, and ask herself, "So, what am I going to wear?" No, two very important elements were working together in Esther's life, which paved the way for her to be fully prepared and in position at just the right moment when God would use her in a magnificent way. *First,* the creative and providential hand of God was on Esther before she was even born. *Second,* Esther was willing to bend her will to the will of God, allowing Him to move her from one significant event in her destiny to the next. The character qualities she would need in that crucial moment were being shaped and molded in her as, one choice at

His Holy Spirit is the only source of bona fide "girl power."

a time, she did the right thing. At every turn, because Esther was obedient, she allowed God to be the Director of her life.

Obedience and Respect

Esther's story of destiny really started when she was a child. You see, she was an orphan—her mother, father, and maybe even her sisters and brothers had been killed, possibly by enemies of the Jews. Because the Jews had been forced to leave their homeland and live in the vast kingdom of Persia, they had to deal with religious and racial prejudice.

After her parents died, Esther went to live with her older cousin Mordecai and his family. She became like a daughter to Mordecai and was devoted to him and obeyed his instructions.

For Esther to fulfill that pivotal moment in her destiny, when she would be used by God to deliver her people from annihilation, it was important for these character traits of respect and obedience to be developed in her. The strength of these traits would eventually lead to her saying *just the right thing* at *just the right time* after she was promoted to *just the right position* to plead with King Xerxes for the lives of her people.

Providence

The opportunity for Esther's "date with destiny" presented itself when King Xerxes became angry with his queen and dethroned her. The main concern here was Queen Vashti's refusal to come when the king called her—it set an example of disrespect that the king's advisors feared might spread into households throughout the kingdom. They suggested that Xerxes hold a sort of pageant to find a woman more worthy of the royal position of queen. The king, of course, liked this idea (what guy wouldn't?).

Obviously, King Xerxes had no idea that God had a plan as well—to use this otherwise worldly contest for His own purposes. Providence was already at work. The road was being paved for God to position *His* girl for a divine moment.

The pageant qualifications were posted: "Wanted: Beautiful Young Virgins."

SET APART FROM THE START

Purity Required

Virginity was one of the qualifications to make it into the first round of this pageant. For a girl to even be considered for the position of queen, she had to have the purity of a virgin.

Esther's purity qualified her for her destiny. In our day and age, some people would consider this requirement politically incorrect at best. Others might say you'd be hard-pressed even to find virgins for the competition. But in Esther's time, physical purity was a huge deal. It was a commentary on a girl's character and the character of her family. An unmarried young girl who was not a virgin would be disowned and labeled contaminated, dirty, and a disgrace to her community. Purity was a valued virtue.

Today it's a different story. Sexual compromise is accepted—and almost expected—in our society. But the high value of purity hasn't changed in God's eyes. The times may have changed, but God hasn't. As His eyes scan the earth for individuals He will move to the next level of preparation in His plan for their lives, His attention is drawn to those who demonstrate lives of purity, virtue, modesty, and discretion.

> He does not take his eyes off the righteous; he enthrones them with kings and exalts them forever.
>
> JOB 36:7

Esther's virginity was an expression of the purity of her heart, mind, and motive. Like Esther, our own inner purity is carried out in the choices we make and in the way we live. I want to say something important here, though: If this discussion about the need for purity has brought conviction in your heart, please be encouraged—you can *always* begin again. If you haven't maintained purity in your life, you aren't forever disqualified from finding God's destiny for your life. God can cleanse you and make you whole again. If you let Him, God will set you apart again, or perhaps for the first time, for His purposes. Remember this: It is never too early or too late to start walking in purity in every area of your life.

Preparation…and the Irresistible Favor of God

Like the other contestants in this beauty pageant, Esther was to be set apart in the palace for a year. There she would be prepared, purified, and beautified before meeting the king and being seriously considered to be his queen. Any blemish she had would be treated with healing agents. Special cosmetics, herbs, and oils were part of this time of intense preparation.

On a physical level, this was a beauty makeover. And what girl doesn't love a makeover? But on a spiritual level, we can see that this was a time of purification and preparation for her promotion to *queen,* and then *advocate.* Like He did with Esther, God is setting girls apart today and preparing them by purifying their hearts, minds, and bodies for purposes yet to be revealed.

God also equipped Esther with the other qualifications needed for her specific destiny. Remember the ad for *Beautiful* Young Virgins? God knew that Esther's youth and outward beauty would capture the king's attention. The Bible says she was "lovely in form and features" (Esther 2:7). But the most attractive thing about Esther was an inner beauty that far outshone the lovely packaging.

In Esther 2:15, we are told that she won the favor of everyone who saw her. Even Hegai, who supervised the young ladies-in-waiting, saw something special in Esther and gave her a private room for her year of preparation. Esther humbly took Hegai's advice about what to take in with her when she visited the king. Obeying Mordecai from the time she was a young child had developed in Esther the heart of a servant who had reverence for those in authority over her. And that kind of character can be very attractive—even irresistible.

Like fine jewels might accessorize her outward beauty, favor decorated Esther's inner life. Because God's favor was resting on Esther as He positioned her for this divine assignment, others couldn't help but be drawn to her.

Handpicked Friends

Hegai approved of Esther so much that he handpicked seven maids to assist, support, and be companions to her during her time of preparation.

These seven Persian women would become such loyal friends to Esther that ultimately they would end up fasting and praying to Esther's

Jewish God for her people. They were also by her side when she was set apart for purification and preparation.

These are the kinds of friends we all should ask God to place in our lives. Friends who will help us in our quest to be set apart, purified, and prepared for His divine purposes. And this is the kind of friend we should seek to be for others. You never know…you just might be God's handpicked maiden friend for someone else.

A Get-Real Girl

As Esther's year of preparation came to an end, her time to go before the king arrived. Each of the young women in the running to become queen could choose to take something into the king's chambers with them, perhaps to capture his attention, entertain, or otherwise make herself memorable to him. The Bible specifies that Esther asked to take *nothing* other than what Hegai suggested (2:15). While Hegai surely knew what might touch the heart of the king, Esther didn't come to this critical moment looking to manipulate, but came authentically, projecting nothing other than *her true self.*

As women, so often we hide behind a mask of some kind or do our little song and dance in an attempt to impress others. We project the image we want people to see in order to hide our insecurity, low self-esteem, anger, or emotional pain. But before we can fully embrace our destiny and God's plan for our lives, we have to "get real" before our King, Jesus. We have to become vulnerable. Because it's in that moment of truth and weakness that God delights in putting a ring on our hand and a robe of righteousness over our shoulders and lifting us to a place of royalty in His court. And isn't that what all God's girls really want?

The Promotion

God's providence and Esther's obedience put Esther in the right place at the right time. And His favor on her made her *irresistible*. You guessed it—the king looked no further. He had found his queen. The crown, the gowns, the sporty new chariot, and the responsibility of this noble position were now Esther's (and she didn't even have to trip the other girls as they strode down the runway or claw their eyes out on her way to the position of Queen Bee). Esther behaved in just the way God had prepared her for, and the promotion followed naturally.

CRISIS BEGINS TO UNFOLD

So Esther was in the palace now, living as the new queen of Persia. But keep in mind that she was still obeying Mordecai's instruction to her that she not reveal her true identity—that she was a Jew. Revealing that secret at this time could've led to some serious consequences for her.

But before Esther even had time to get cozy in the safety of her new royal position, an evil plot began to unfold….

Just when Esther might've started settling on the idea that being queen of Persia *was* her destiny, she began to realize that God had a much bigger plan. All along, God had been planning to turn an enemy's evil plot into a miraculous blessing for the Jewish people. Only God could've known in advance that a need for a young woman who was adorned with character, courage, and compassion—and had the favor of the king—was about to arise.

The details of Esther's life are a wonderful example of the supernatural ways in which God fulfills His plan and purpose by putting people into certain positions, circumstances, and events. Some people see this divine providence as being like the pieces of fabric that are organized and sewn into a beautiful and intricate quilt.

Even before Haman, the king's right-hand man, got mad at Mordecai, God knew that this self-serving and ambitious assistant would rear his ugly head and become an enemy of God's people. He knew that when the king elevated Haman higher than all the other noblemen, Haman's ego would ultimately get the best of him. God also knew that Mordecai, who was faithful to God, wouldn't kneel down before Haman. Mordecai wouldn't even think of expressing worship toward someone other than God.

A Test of Character

So when Mordecai refused to bow down to him, Haman became so angry that he decided to take out his fury on all the Jewish people in the kingdom. He concocted a deceptive scheme and convinced King Xerxes to pass a law that would lead to the massacre of all the Jews in the kingdom. The king agreed to Haman's proposal, but he had no idea that he was signing the death sentence for his own wife, Queen Esther.

At this point, Esther's resolve, courage, and trust in God were put to the test like never before. Mordecai sent a message to Esther, begging her to go to the king and plead for mercy on behalf of the Jews. Here, for the first time, we see Esther hesitate in response to an instruction from Mordecai. She probably felt a bit uncertain in her position as queen. After all, the king hadn't called for her in over a month. And, worst-case, barging in on him uninvited could lead to death.

When Esther still wasn't seeing clearly that her destiny could be fulfilled in this crisis—or the important role she could play in this critical moment in history—Mordecai hit her with this eye-opener:

> "Do not think that because you are in the king's house you alone of all the Jews will escape. For if you remain silent at this time, relief and deliverance for the Jews will arise from another place, but you and your father's family will perish…."

The conclusion of this well-known passage surely must have jolted Esther into reality:

"And who knows but that you have come to royal position *for such a time as this?*"

ESTHER 4:13–14, ITALICS MINE

In his passionate plea, Mordecai pointed out that *this was a destiny moment for Esther.* God may have strategically positioned her as queen just so she could approach King Xerxes and ask him to have mercy on her people. Even though Mordecai had suggested all along that Esther's destiny perhaps was to be the person God used to bring "relief and deliverance for the Jews" (v. 14), Esther still had a choice to make. Would she take the step that just might be the fulfillment of a master plan orchestrated by God? Would she believe Mordecai's words—that putting her life on the line now was the only way to preserve it later?

An Esther Moment ("Aha!"..."Oh no!")

As Esther began to realize the gravity of her predicament, she had what I call an "Esther moment." An "Aha!" moment is quickly followed by an "Oh no!" response. First, there is the "Aha! *Now* I see that this situation I'm dealing with is about more than just me. It's a God thing!" Then right on the heels of this realization comes the "Oh no! This may *cost me* something. Am I willing to give up my pride, my reputation, my acceptance by others, my comfortable lifestyle, or even my very life to do what God is asking?" When an Esther moment happens in your own life, it is *your opportunity* to choose faith over fear and to be God's courageous girl.

For her pivotal destiny moment to fully unfold, Esther had a choice to make.

$$Courage = Faith > Fear$$

Okay…back to Esther. 🖐

Mordecai gave her the options: She could choose to hold back and not act, but God would still raise up *someone* to do what He had destined *her* to do. (He's God—He'll get the job done with or without us!)

Or she could act.

One of the key lessons we learn from the life of Esther is that she could've either stepped toward or walked away from this moment. She could've either fulfilled her God-given destiny of being a part of God's larger plan for His people, or not.

Ever been there? I sure have. Over the years there have been critical moments when I faced my fear and boldly stepped into my destiny. *But* at other times I've hung my head in regret after I backed away in fear and disobeyed God at a very crucial and pivotal point in my life. The good news is that God *always* brings us to another destiny moment. But each time He gives us these opportunities, we are the ones who choose whether to walk into our date with destiny.

Esther's years of character preparation had all been leading up to *this* "Aha!"…"Oh no!" moment. Emboldened by the realization that she had been positioned to be God's agent in the situation, she leaped into action. Esther chose to stand between the death sentence and her people. She chose to fight for what was right. Esther the Queen chose to accept her promotion to Esther the Advocate. She chose to take up a cause that was much bigger than her—one that could even jeopardize her own safety and well being—and rise up into God's call!

"IF I DIE, I DIE"

As Esther rose to the call, she expressed a boldness and spiritual authority we haven't seen in her before. First she called on all the Jews in the land to come together and fast:

"Go, gather together all the Jews…and fast for me. Do not eat
or drink for three days…. I and my maids will fast as you do.
When this is done, I will go to the king, even though it is
against the law. And if I perish, I perish."

ESTHER 4:16

Now here's a really cool thing: Esther was humble enough to
recognize that she needed God's favor, wisdom, power, and protection
to pull off this mission. So first thing, she humbled herself before God
by determining to fast from food and drink for three days so that she
could turn her full attention to Him. And then she asked others to join
her and her maids in this fast. By doing that, she humbled herself
before her people, admitting that she couldn't do it alone and that she
needed them.

Courage

After spending three days in prayer preparation, Esther put on her
royal robes and stood in the inner court of the palace, where the king
could see her (Esther 5:1). Just as Esther's royal robes represented her
royal position as queen, our royal robes represent Christ's righteousness
in us. A beautiful picture of our spiritual garments can be seen in the
following Scripture:

I delight greatly in the LORD; my soul rejoices in my God. For
he has clothed me with garments of salvation and arrayed me
in a robe of righteousness, as a bridegroom adorns his head
like a priest, and as a bride adorns herself with her jewels.

ISAIAH 61:10

Although Esther was wearing royal robes, that doesn't mean she
just barged into the king's throne room and demanded an audience.
Perhaps her favor with the king was waning because she hadn't been

invited into his presence for an entire month. But Esther didn't shrink back in fear either. (Now that's what I call God-given girl power!) She simply stood in the court and waited for the king to acknowledge her.

And of course he did. The king noticed Esther standing there, respectfully waiting, honoring his position of authority. Pleased with her grace and dignity, he held out his scepter. Her life had been spared—he had invited her in.

Esther must've been trembling. But this elegant young lady courageously stood her ground in God's purposes, even after the king asked her why she sought his presence and told her that she could have whatever she wanted, even if it meant giving her half of the kingdom. (If it were me, I might have laid it all out right then and there when I saw that he was in such a generous mood.) But Esther, fresh off a period of fasting, was more discerning about how to carry out God's plan. Instead of making her request right away, she invited him and his most honored nobleman, Haman, to a banquet she had already prepared.

Hospitality, Coming Up!

That's right, Esther wanted to include Haman, of all people! Can you imagine inviting your enemy into your home and serving him? Now that would really require some inner strength.

In this day and age, gestures of hospitality are often thought of as being too *girlie* and not worth the hassle. Not for Esther though. At the Lord's leading, she must have realized that inviting people into your personal space and serving them is often just what is needed to open the door to genuine communication and relationship.

As Esther's gift of hospitality increased her favor with the king, the stage was being set for her to overcome evil with good. The king was delighted by his queen's generous and kind spirit. Again, he asked her to make her request. Again, he guaranteed that he would give her what she wanted, even if it meant half his kingdom.

The situation seemed to scream for the unveiling of Esther's true identity and the concern that was weighing heavily on her heart. But Esther discerned that she must wait. The time to speak with boldness hadn't yet come, so she invited both the king and Haman back for another banquet the next day.

Waiting for God's Perfect Timing

Oh, what a difference a day can make!

The scene at this second dinner was much different. In the twenty-four hours following the first banquet, Haman's pride had gotten the best of him. First, he got so caught up in his boasting and his anger toward Mordecai that he built gallows from which to hang Mordecai for not bowing down to him. Then, when the king asked Haman how to honor a man who had served him faithfully, Haman assumed the king was referring to him and suggested elaborate methods of honoring this person. But to Haman's surprise (and disgust, I'm sure), King Xerxes was asking for suggestions on how to honor *Mordecai,* who had once saved him from assassination. Even worse, the king then commanded Haman to carry out the grand public display of appreciation for Mordecai, the very man he had planned to hang. I guess that explains the saying "Pride goes before a fall."

Finally, at the second banquet, the king again asked Queen Esther to make her request. He again guaranteed that he would give her what she wanted, even up to half his kingdom. *This time* Esther discerned that the perfect timing of the Lord had come, and she spoke with boldness:

> "If I have found favor with you, O king, and if it pleases your majesty, grant me my life—this is my petition. And spare my people—this is my request. For I and my people have been sold for destruction and slaughter and annihilation."

ESTHER 7:3–4

What was this?!

King Xerxes was shocked that anyone would threaten Esther and her people. Who would do such a thing to his precious Queen Esther? When Esther told the king that Haman was the man behind all of it, the king's eyes were opened to the truth. Ultimately, Haman was hanged on the very gallows he had built for Mordecai, Esther was given all of Haman's possessions, and Mordecai was honored and given Haman's position serving the king.

And the destiny moment? The Jews were liberated and given the right to defend themselves. Celebrations took place throughout the kingdom to honor them. People of all races even converted and became Jews at the news of what happened. To this day, the Jewish holiday Purim is celebrated to remember this victory that came through the young Queen Esther.

Esther had indeed found favor in the eyes of King Xerxes. The road to this girl becoming first Esther the Queen and then Esther the Advocate was paved by the character qualities that she humbly and reverently allowed God to build in her and then use for His purposes. As she stepped into one providential opportunity after another, her destiny to turn a potential national crisis into a miraculous deliverance was sealed. What Satan meant for evil, God used for His good.

When people witness our character and courage for Christ, they become curious. They want to know more about this God who is obviously inspiring us and decorating our lives. Let the life of Esther and the lives of the modern-day Esthers highlighted in this book inspire you to have the same impact on your world. Perhaps you were born and brought to this place in your life *for such a time as this.*

Positioned by God as Advocates for Others

savingarrows

For hours now, Melissa and Christin had been taking turns peeking through the little hole in the fence. Sure, they hardly ever knew if anyone changed her mind when hour after hour, week after week, month after month, they called out, "Excuse me, ma'am, can I talk to you for just a minute? Can I offer you some literature?" But how could they not keep trying? After all, what if just one baby's life was saved because they were standing out there?

After praying together, Melissa and Christin again took their posts in the back of the clinic, behind the fence that surrounded the parking lot. Their friend Danielle stood out front, near the entrance to the parking lot. So far, today had been a little easier than some of the other days over the years. At least it wasn't raining, freezing cold, or so hot that they were dripping with sweat. And the cops hadn't shouted at them through a megaphone. And no one had cussed them out yet.

As Danielle handed out pamphlets to people driving in or walking up to the parking lot, she remembered when she and Melissa had prayed for more kids to come work at the clinics with them. For one thing, most of the young women going to the clinics to have abortions were teenagers and were more open to talking to someone their own age. They seemed to turn away in shame when they were approached by adults.

After being the only two their age going to the clinics on Saturdays—and every day during the summer—for so long, Danielle and Melissa had gotten kind of lonely. They had been going with their parents to pro-life events since they were young children. Since then, they had often wondered if they were the only kids dedicated to saving the lives of the unborn.

The girls had often wondered if they were the only kids dedicated to saving the lives of the unborn.

It was so great that several other teenagers and college kids had joined the group they had formed, called Saving Arrows. Wow, God had really put together quite a group. Of course, the kids with pink hair, with pierced noses or lips, or wearing chains really stood out. But it was also hard not to notice the different races—black, white, Hispanic, and Asian.

Their hope that others would join them had really begun to build when they organized a couple of youth rallies at a local church. Christin had been one of the twenty or so teens that started going to the clinics with them after that first rally. Looking back, it was hard to believe that Christin had once told Melissa that she thought Melissa and her family were crazy for going to pro-life events all the time.

As Danielle stood near the clinic parking lot and thanked God for putting this eclectic group together, she saw Melissa running toward her. "A girl has changed her mind!" Danielle's heart started racing as she began to comprehend what Melissa was saying—a girl had changed her mind about aborting her baby!

Thank You sooo much, God! Thank You for rescuing one of your little ones. And thank You for saving this mother from the heartache she'd have had when she later realized the truth about what abortion really is…that it really is the killing of the most innocent and helpless little ones created in Your image.

Melissa and Christin would later tell Danielle how this rescue had unfolded and how they had almost missed the opportunity altogether. If it hadn't been for a little hole in the green plastic that was woven through the chain-link fence, it would've been impossible to see any of the women once they drove into the parking lot, which was posted with a No Trespassing sign and was hidden behind the eight-foot-high privacy fence.

The hole in the fence was just big enough for the girls to peer through with one eye. People would often get confused as they walked by and heard, "Psst! Psst! Over here! May I talk to you for just a minute?"

The puzzled girls would look up at the sky, behind cars, and all around them and ask, "Hey, where's that voice coming from?" Quite a few would even say, "Hey, where are you? What do you want?" Sometimes it seemed like they thought maybe it was the voice of God…*trying to stop them.* And He was!

But rather than speaking to these young women like He spoke to Moses, from a fire-engulfed bush (see Exodus 3), God was speaking through Danielle, Melissa, and Christin—three modern-day Esthers who had become advocates for life. They chose to spend entire days not at the mall, but at abortion clinics, taking turns straining to watch for someone, anyone, to walk close enough to hear them call out.

The parking lot had been fairly full that day, and the girls had slipped literature through the hole to quite a few people. Some had been husbands or boyfriends waiting while their wives or girlfriends were inside.

Melissa and Christin had noticed a woman sitting in her car for what seemed like a long time. The girls assumed she was just waiting to give someone a ride home, so they didn't pay much attention to her. As they visited with each other, Melissa peeked through the hole…just in time to catch a glimpse of the young woman hurrying toward the clinic. And she looked like she was about to cry.

Knowing that she had only a few seconds to get the girl's attention, Melissa called out, "Excuse me…can we offer you some literature?" The girl stopped in her tracks, like someone had put a brick wall in front of her. She spun around and started looking for where the voice was coming from.

Again, Melissa called out, "May I give you something?"

When the young woman realized the voice was coming from the hole in the fence, she nodded and walked toward it.

She unrolled the pamphlet Melissa had poked through the hole. On the first page was a picture of an unborn child. As soon as the woman saw it, she burst into tears. Turning around, she rushed toward her car—and away from the clinic!

The providence of God and their obedience had converged for an eternal purpose.

Realizing what was happening, Melissa ran to the front of the building, where she knew the woman would be exiting the parking lot. Her heart raced as she dialed the Crisis Pregnancy Center on her cell phone.

"Can I…I have someone I'd like to bring in. Is that okay?"

"Well, actually, we're closing. But you know I'll stay open for you, Melissa," said the familiar voice on the other end.

Near tears now, Melissa exclaimed, "Thank you! Oh, thank you so much!"

Just then, Melissa saw the young woman's car coming toward her. She motioned for her to stop. Leaning into the window, Melissa said, "Hi. I can hop in my car right now and drive over to the Crisis Pregnancy Center with you. They can help you there. Would you like to follow me?"

The girl nodded and said okay.

Melissa felt a sense of exhilaration as she realized that she and the others were part of a God thing in the life of this young woman and her unborn child. The providence of God and their obedience had converged for an eternal purpose. Melissa ran to her car and signaled for the girl to follow her. As she drove toward the center, Melissa checked her rearview mirror and called CPC again to let them know that she and the young woman were on their way.

"What's her name?" the intake counselor asked.

"I don't know. I don't have a clue…she's just following me in her car!"

As they parked their cars and headed to the door of CPC, Melissa smiled at the young woman and said, "This is the place, the Crisis Pregnancy Center. Hi, I'm Melissa."

"Thanks so much for coming over here with me. My name's Latisha."

Melissa put her hand on the girl's shoulder. "I'm so glad to meet you, Latisha. Let's go in together."

They sat silently in the waiting room while Latisha began filling out some paperwork. After a few minutes of settling in, Latisha said, "I'll be okay now. I'll be fine waiting by myself."

Melissa said good-bye, got in her car, and began the drive back to the abortion clinic. As Melissa thought about their brief but emotional encounter, she began to pray:

Oh Lord, help Latisha stay strong in her decision not to abort her baby. Put a love in her heart for this baby that will not be swayed

*by anyone in her family or any friends who might try to convince
her to go back and have the abortion. Thank You for the wonderful
plans You have for the life of this child.*

Later, when Danielle, Melissa, and Christin talked about all that
had happened that day, they were amazed at how the chance to save
that baby's life was almost missed. They *almost* hadn't gone that day
because they all had homework and exams to prepare for. Christin and
Melissa *almost* hadn't seen the young woman get out of her car and
head toward the clinic. Latisha had *almost* made it to the clinic door
before she heard Melissa calling out to her. And the Crisis Pregnancy
Center had *almost* closed when Melissa called.

Reflecting on what almost didn't happen, Melissa said, "You know,
we could have missed something huge. We could be missing out on
accomplishing something really great for God or making a difference in
someone else's life." The girls talked about how many opportunities
might be missed when we don't pay attention to the Holy Spirit's
nudging.

God had turned an *almost* into an *actuality.*

A WONDERFUL SURPRISE

A couple of months later, the providence of God was again in motion,
as it had been that day at the clinic. I had been invited to be the emcee
at a fund-raiser for Crisis Pregnancy Centers (CPC).

This was a large event, held in the grand ballroom of Founder's Inn
in Virginia Beach. Hundreds of people were in attendance, sitting at
splendidly decorated tables. I was seated at the head table so that I
could introduce the speakers that evening.

When I got there, I was disappointed to learn that Alan Keyes, the
keynote speaker for the evening, couldn't make it because he had been

in a minor car accident. In his place would be Pastor Johnny Hunter, a man with many credits to his name and an advocate for pro-life issues who had come as a supporter of CPC. Dr. Keyes's absence meant that Pastor Hunter would be taking the lead that evening. None of us had any idea that God was setting His own agenda for the night.

God's surprise began to unfold later in the evening when I introduced a young lady who had been a client of CPC. I listened as this expectant young mother shared her story of how the center had helped her. Through tears, she expressed how distraught she had been to discover a couple of months earlier that she was pregnant. She already had two children and didn't think she could handle the burden of caring for a third. She had gone to an abortion clinic intending to abort her baby.

She hadn't gone through with the abortion and was going to have her baby.

She went on to explain that as she was about to walk into the clinic, someone had called out to her and handed her some literature through a little hole in the fence surrounding the parking lot. And because of that, she hadn't gone through with the abortion and was going to have her baby.

While she shared her story, a couple of girls quietly approached Pastor Hunter and whispered something to him. A big smile began to spread across his face. As the girls returned to their seats, this beautiful and articulate young woman at the podium went on to explain how grateful she was for all the help she had received through CPC.

Everyone applauded as Latisha left the stage and returned to her seat. It appeared that this young woman's contribution to the event that evening was over.

If you would like to volunteer at a CPC near you, or if you are in the middle of a crisis pregnancy, log on to www.optionline.org, or call the Option Line at 1-800-395-HELP.

Pastor Hunter walked to the microphone. Now, he's one of those wonderful black preachers who can masterfully weave and color a story. So he began to lay out this story about how God had ordained this evening and how something was happening that was not on the agenda.

Pastor Hunter explained that his daughter Danielle, her two friends Melissa and Christin, and other young people in a group called Saving Arrows consistently went to the same abortion clinic Latisha had referred to. In fact, he had seen them poke literature through that little hole in the fence. So when Latisha told her story, he had a pretty good idea who had given her the literature and escorted her to CPC.

"Latisha, would you like to meet the girls who were on the other side of the fence that day?"

Her face lit up with surprise and she nodded slowly.

"Girls, come on up here," he said, as he looked toward the back of the banquet hall.

A soft chatter swept across the banquet hall as people began to realize that they were witnessing a God moment. There wasn't a dry eye in the room as the three girls made their way from the back of the banquet hall up to the stage. Here were three teenage girls, as average-looking as any other teens you might see, but there was something very different about them.

Instead of hanging out at the mall or doing other things kids their age normally do on Saturdays, they had regularly and faithfully tried to defend the lives of preborn babies. Much in the same way Esther of the Bible stood in the gap for the life of her people, these young warrior princesses were doing all they could to stop the imminent deaths that loomed just fifteen to twenty steps away—the distance between where the pregnant girls parked their cars and the doorway into the clinic.

Because of these girls, Latisha was spared the awful emotional pain of abortion and her baby had been given its rightful chance at life.

Hundreds of guests in the banquet hall froze in amazement as we watched Pastor Hunter join Latisha's hand with Melissa's, Danielle's, and Christin's in a tearful reunion.

This is how I first became acquainted with these young women. The encounter is also what inspired me to write this book. When I saw the mantle of Esther on these three girls, I knew that they, and others like them, would inspire young women to rise up into God's call for them to be modern-day Esthers for their generation.

SAVING EVEN MORE ARROWS

When I spoke with the girls again recently, I was pleased and not at all surprised to learn that after Danielle, Melissa, and Christin moved to other states for college and ministry, each girl began developing new chapters of Saving Arrows. Christin's little sister Heather—who was a whopping *fifteen years old* at the time—was now heading up the original Virginia Beach chapter.

As I interviewed each of them, I was incredibly impressed at how mature, articulate, and passionate these girls were for their ages. Heather told me that she was only eleven when she started going out to the clinics with her sister. Now, four years later, she is leading the fifteen to twenty young people who make up the original Saving Arrows chapter.

While Heather is holding down the fort in Virginia Beach, her sister Christin has launched a new Saving Arrows chapter at the college she attends in Tennessee. It has quickly grown to nearly fifty members. And when Danielle moved to North Carolina with her parents, she went to work setting up a new chapter and going out to the abortion clinics there.

Melissa has taken Saving Arrows to a national level. She told me that she has a vision for every Christian church to be part of making sure that pro-life rescue teams are posted during the hours of operation at every abortion clinic in America. As we talked, she told me that today's generation of young people has been impacted more by abortion than any other generation since the U.S. Supreme Court handed down the two rulings over thirty years ago legalizing abortion and resulting in the deaths of more than 42 million preborn babies.[1]

"Because it was our brothers, our sisters, and our best friends who were killed before they were even born, we have a double responsibility," Melissa explained. "We need to speak for the third of our generation that has died by abortion, and we need to make sure we don't do the same to the next generation."

As Melissa spoke, my thoughts were taken back to a movie that many of us watch every Christmas season: *It's a Wonderful Life*. In this movie, Jimmy Stewart's character is shown what his life and his town would have been like if he had never been born. When protected by his compassion and self-sacrifice, the town remained a charming and thriving community. But without his influence, it was reduced to a breeding ground for bars and strip clubs, and the town was swallowed up by a greedy property owner.

As I thought about this while Christin and I talked, I began to wonder, *How much richer would our lives be if those 42 million people were with us today? How might they have impacted the world…and our lives?* I once heard someone ask the question: What if the person who might have discovered a cure for cancer was aborted before he or she was even born? *So many* things in our world might be different if the lives of aborted babies had been saved.

Saving Arrows:
If you are interested in starting a chapter of Saving Arrows in your community, e-mail Melissa at savingarrows@hotmail.com.

MODERN-DAY ESTHERS

Unfortunately, we can't change the past. We can, however, learn from it—if we choose to. We can also learn from the modern-day Esthers who are choosing to respond *right now* to God's calling on their lives.

The girls of Saving Arrows are confident that they have been prepared and positioned by God to stand between life and death for preborn babies. In fact, Saving Arrows was birthed in prayer. After weighing the idea of forming a group for some time, Melissa asked the Lord to give her a name for it only if He really wanted them to start it up formally. As she prayed about it one day, the Lord led her to a Bible passage that made the name "Saving Arrows" leap out at her. She knew it was time to move forward:

Sons are a heritage from the LORD, children a reward from him. Like *arrows* in the hands of a warrior are sons born in one's youth. Blessed is the man whose quiver is full of them. They will not be put to shame when they contend with their enemies in the gate.

PSALM 127:3–5, ITALICS MINE

These young women are so committed to saving "arrows"—to saving sons and daughters, which are "a heritage from the LORD."

Many of the characteristics in Esther can also be seen in the members of Saving Arrows and in the lives of the other young ladies we'll be taking a look at throughout the book. I hope and pray that something about how God is using these modern-day Esthers will inspire you to take up a cause that is bigger than you—to get outside yourself and say:

> *God, I believe that You can*
> *work through me now,*
> *while I am young.*
> *What are You calling me to*
> *do for You today?*
> *How can I be an Esther*
> *to this generation?*

chapter three

A Lifestyle of Purity

rebecca st.james

When I think of young women whose lives exhibit the qualities and strength of character we see in Esther, Rebecca St. James quickly comes to mind. And when I think of her, a young woman who has been raised up by God to set a standard for purity, the word that most jumps out at me is *virtuous*. Rebecca's passion for God and her burden to inspire others to remain sexually pure until marriage comes through loud and clear in her ministry *and* in her life. The word *virtuous*—being morally excellent, righteous, chaste, pure in thought and act, and modest—is an old-fashioned word, but one that we need to embrace again in our culture.[1]

I think *virtuous* best describes Rebecca, because for more than a decade she has taken the steps necessary to make sure her walk matches her talk. In the first few paragraphs of a feature article Deanna Broxton wrote about Rebecca in *Christian Music Planet*, she gives a good summary of how consistently virtuous Rebecca is in all aspects of her life:

There's something extraordinary about Rebecca St. James. It's not that she is a Grammy Award-winning vocalist; or that she recorded her first worship album when she was just 13, in her native Australia. It's not even that she has six albums (actually seven now) to her credit, and is one of the most admired women in Christian music. No, simply put, 25-year-old St. James is special because she has a sweet humble spirit, and depth of spirituality that cannot be hid under a bushel. It shines in the warmth of her smile and easy laughter, or when she reminisces about taking care of needy children in Romania and India, or even in the way she earnestly seeks God every day.

As the daughter of a Christian concert promoter, St. James may have literally grown up in the music industry, but the limelight has not tainted her, nor do her musical successes define her. Instead, the mission of her ministry and music are clear.

"I want to point people to Jesus," St. James explains. "I want to share His hope with them. I have seen such a need—our world is hungering and starving for truth, for hope and for God. So, that is what I want to give them."

Yet, in order to point people to Christ, St. James must nurture her own relationship with God by taking time out of her hectic schedule. During a recent six-month sabbatical, she sought God, allowing Him to speak to her heart.[2]

So how has this young woman, whom music fans have voted as the top woman in Christian music today, continued to wave her purity banner so high that it flies right in the face of what our culture is saying to and about women?[3]

COMMITTED TO A LIFETIME OF PURITY

Rebecca's commitment to staying sexually pure until she marries jelled when she was sixteen years old. She had been asked to sing at a True Love Waits rally at a park in Peoria, Illinois. This was her first exposure to the True Love Waits movement. She already knew about and appreciated the benefits of staying sexually pure until marriage and knew that she wanted to stay pure until she married, but after hearing the speaker share on the topic of purity, she knew she needed to make a *real* commitment. So along with several hundred other young people, she formally committed to staying sexually pure. She is now among the ranks of over a million young people who have signed covenant cards stating that they will remain abstinent until they enter a biblical marriage relationship.

In her book *Wait for Me,* Rebecca describes how the commitment she made that evening has unfolded into a passion to inspire others to do the same: "From that day on I have felt a passionate tug on my heart to share God's wonderful way, His beautiful protection of marriage— sexual abstinence until the wedding day."[4]

But Rebecca's commitment to purity goes beyond simply remaining abstinent. More than anything, she wants to glorify God by living every area of her life *His way.* Along with not wanting to live with regrets later, the true desire of Rebecca's heart is to be able to look back on her life and say, "God, I really sought to please You in every way, and even though I've failed on occasion, I really sought to keep my standards high and to follow after You with all my heart."

Worldwide Accountability

After Rebecca made the True Love Waits commitment, she immediately told her friends and family about it. She also started talking about her commitment at her concerts. As a teenager talking to other teens, she started sharing the message, "Hey, let's stand together on this—you're not alone." And now that she is in her midtwenties, she sees her role as that of a big sister or older friend who is still standing with young people and saying, "Live God's way—it's awesome!"

Her enthusiasm for inspiring other people to live God's way is a natural expression of her love for Him, as well as the result of God's gentle nudge in her life for her to do this.

As you can probably imagine, being under the watchful eye of the thousands of people who come to hear her sing, having her face on magazine covers, being a guest on television shows, and releasing a book and a song about purity is a big responsibility.

Rebecca takes her role as a mentor very seriously. But even if she weren't in the limelight, her commitment to the Lord would still be her top priority. Her personal relationship with the Lord—rather than the expectations or opinions of others—is what motivates her to stay on track spiritually.

So what's it like to have millions of people watching you after you have taken up the banner of the message of purity, stating your commitment publicly and encouraging others to live God's way? When I asked Rebecca about this, she told me that instead of feeling overly pressured by the many people who watch her life, she feels like she has millions of accountability partners all around the world.

Her family and friends also help her toe the line when it comes to purity. They pray for her and encourage her to keep her heart and life centered on God. When it comes to accountability, she confides most in her mom and her two closest friends, Karleen and Stacey. She and her brothers also talk often about relationships because they too are at that stage in life when they are either courting or considering it.

Rebecca's dad is also a big part of her life. She laughed when I told her that I have often heard it said that people don't know Rebecca St. James very long before meeting her dad. He plays the dual role of being both her father and her manager. She sees his guidance and protection as one of the ways God takes care of her. She told me she believes that God gives fathers and other family members the mantle, or responsibility and function, of being a woman's protectors until she marries and the role is passed on to her husband. I couldn't agree with her more!

Purposeful Courting

Rebecca recognizes the need for extra caution when it comes to her own romantic interests. She really didn't date during her teen years. Yes, she did have crushes when she was a teen, but she was twenty years old before she felt like she was actually courting someone. She said this was partly because of being on the road so much, but also because she sees no reason for a girl to have to deal with sexual pressure early on, when she's not even close to thinking about marriage. As far as she's concerned, dating before you're ready to consider marriage is just asking for trouble. And I agree. Girls and guys going out in groups is much safer, especially before you're old enough to marry.

Rebecca told me that she thinks it's important for people not to have a user mentality when they date or court. She is quick to point out that if a girl can't imagine a guy as a possible lifelong mate, she shouldn't even consider dating him. When we were talking about this, Rebecca said that her friend Josh Harris's term "purposeful courting" sums up her own view—that romantic relationships should be a way of purposefully exploring the possibility of marrying the person you are courting. In *Boy Meets Girl,* Josh describes the difference between *purposeless* and *purposeful* romantic relationships like this:

> I happen to like the term *courtship*. It's old-fashioned, but it evokes romance and chivalry. I use it to describe not a set of rules, but that special season in a romance where a man and

woman are seriously weighing the possibility of marriage. I think it's helpful to distinguish between undefined and directionless romances (what I said goodbye to) and a romantic relationship that is purposefully headed towards marriage.[5]

Why is Rebecca so strong on this point? Because when a girl is dating a guy for any reason other than to pursue marriage, she is using him for something—maybe to have someone to take her places or to give her a sense of security and self-worth.

If you really think about it, it's actually kind of mean for a girl to use someone to take her to fun or expensive places! Shouldn't a girl's security and sense of self-worth come from her relationship with the Lord and not from whether she has a date every Friday night? We'll take a more in-depth look at this idea a little later.

Personal Boundaries

Rebecca is committed to dating or courting only men who have the same values she does. But even with those personal boundaries in place, she recognizes that she isn't invincible. She knows that her true strength, courage, and purity can only come from the Lord. And this falls right in line with Scripture: "So, if you think you are standing firm, be careful that you don't fall!" (1 Corinthians 10:12).

Because she knows that outer purity is actually a by-product of inner purity, Rebecca sets aside time each day to be alone with God, to seek Him and develop inner purity. But even with millions of accountability partners and the ultimate Accountability Partner—the Lord—she can't help but remember the number of people committed to purity that she has seen stumble. To Rebecca, seeing this happen to couples is like a big warning sign that says: Be wise—don't get yourself into situations outside the safety zone (which we'll talk about a little later in the chapter).

Purity Reborn

If you're reading this and feeling regrets because you have already slipped outside that place of safety and protection and have exposed yourself to sexual sin, listen up!

God doesn't want you to live in the shame and pain of the past. If you stop sinning and sincerely ask God to forgive you and cleanse you from your mistakes, He will. That's the incredible thing about God. He can make you into a new creature—in your heart, mind, soul, *and* body. Girls who have made mistakes in the past have been able to take great comfort in reclaiming their purity and becoming "born-again virgins."

God doesn't want you to live in the shame and pain of the past.

Be aware, though: If you have prematurely aroused the sexual desires deep within you, it can be very hard to suppress that curiosity and appetite. But with God's help, you can once again become a lady-in-waiting. All the more reason to take determined steps to put protective advice like Rebecca's into action in your life.

True Love Does Wait

The True Love Waits pledge that Rebecca took now reads: "Believing that true love waits, I make a commitment to God, myself, my family, my friends, my future mate, and my future children to a lifetime of purity including sexual abstinence from this day until the day I enter a biblical marriage relationship."[6]

Take a few minutes to read the pledge again. What is God saying to you as you consider those words? Do you feel the same way Rebecca did so long ago? Do you feel like you need to make a real and formal commitment to this?

One way to make this commitment official—to sign on the dotted line, so to speak—is to sign a pledge card on-line at TrueLoveWaits.com. No matter how you decide to formalize your stand on purity, making a commitment to God and to yourself is the first step. The second step is being accountable to others, which will help you keep that commitment. So be sure to tell your family and friends that you are also committing to them that you will guard your purity.

And then celebrate your decision!

Log on to TrueLoveWaits.com. Be counted by joining the thousands of other people who have made a formal pledge to a lifetime of purity.

PLAYING IT SAFE

For Rebecca, playing it safe when it comes to purity includes being careful about what her eyes see, her ears hear, and her mind thinks. She encourages young and old alike—single people and married people—to guard their minds and hearts closely. Sex is a sacred gift from God that is reserved only for uniting a husband and wife. Rebecca knows this, so she steers clear of anything that presents sex flippantly or grotesquely. She is quick to warn people about things like movies or television programs that might arouse them, lead them to think about sex in a degrading way, or present sex as something unsacred.

As for music, yep, you guessed it—she listens mostly to Christian music. For one thing, she wants to protect her mind from thoughts or lyrics that might point her in an ungodly direction. Plus, she wants to protect other people by setting an example of someone who is listening to things that are pure and of God.

Rebecca's safety zone also includes keeping her mind soaked in the Word so that she will focus on things that are pure, stay set apart for Him, fix her eyes on Jesus, and center her values on His will and the eternal prize of heaven. To sum up this approach, she often refers to this Scripture:

> You'll do best by filling your minds and meditating on things true, noble, reputable, authentic, compelling, gracious—the best, not the worst; the beautiful, not the ugly; things to praise, not things to curse. Put into practice what you learned from me, what you heard and saw and realized. Do that, and God, who makes everything work together, will work you into his most excellent harmonies.
>
> PHILIPPIANS 4:8–9, *THE MESSAGE*

To help others keep their minds pure before the Lord, Rebecca is careful about what she wears onstage, making sure that her outfits are funky but modest. She doesn't want to cause men to stumble by thinking of her in a sexual way, so she avoids wearing clothes that show a large amount of skin—outfits that are too tight, show cleavage, or bare her midriff, upper chest, or back. She avoids short skirts and shorts.

In addition to protecting guys' eyes and thoughts, Rebecca also wants to be an example to other women. She said that many girls have thanked her for dressing modestly or have told her that no one had ever explained to them that wearing short skirts or showing a lot of skin causes guys to stumble. Even though it may seem difficult to find funky, modern, cool clothes that are also modest, she is determined to hold the line in this area—and you can too!

Rebecca also plays it safe by avoiding circumstances that might be either unsafe for her or misunderstood by others. For example, she won't ride alone in a car with a member of the opposite sex when she's out on the road. This includes car rides to wherever she will be singing—if the runner is a man and he arrives alone, she will ask him to go back and get a woman. However, Rebecca will ride alone with a guy who is a trusted friend or someone she is courting who shares her values.

Be wise—don't get yourself into situations outside the safety zone!

Rebecca also avoids being behind closed doors with a guy. If she's in a situation where she is alone with a guy for more than a brief period of time, she props the door open to guard against any appearance of impropriety.

Glow in Virtue

These may sound like unrealistic standards—given the world we live in, that is. One example of worldly (or ungodly) standards is the way young women dress and act on the recently popularized reality TV shows. To gain the attention of millions of viewers or to boost ratings, they dress scantily and seduce guys, who fall right into the lust trap.

Rebecca's virtuous behavior and lifestyle are the very opposite of what these shows and other media messages present as being "normal." And this is what makes Rebecca stand out as a real modern-day Esther and a refreshing contrast to what pop culture defines as the norm. When you think about it, being modest and living honorably sure haven't hurt Rebecca's ratings. Instead of dwindling because of her commitment to living virtuously, Rebecca's record sales and the number of people attending her concerts have only grown! God's favor is evident in her life and ministry.

Too often, though, even Christian girls reflect the ungodly world more than they reflect Christ. But rather than joining in with the works of darkness and reflecting an ungodly world, we should be reflections of the character of Christ through the light of our pure lifestyles. So be inspired to glow in virtue and grow in the favor of God. Remember, like Jesus describes Himself in John 8:23, we are supposed to be in this world but not of it.

> Have nothing to do with the fruitless deeds of darkness, but rather expose them.
>
> EPHESIANS 5:11

Under the Protection of Loved Ones

While most young people can't wait to get out from under the watchful eye of mom and dad, Rebecca chooses the added safety of living within the physical and spiritual protection of her parents' home. She tells the story of her short-lived experience of "getting out on her own." She bought a little house, fixed it up, and was all excited about spreading her wings. But it didn't take long for her to feel vulnerable. After several months in her own place, she decided to move back home with her parents.

Rebecca thinks that sticking close to friends and family is also important for couples who are dating. In fact, she thinks that couples are heading into a danger zone when they spend too much time alone together. For one thing, the relationship may become emotionally charged before they've really had a chance to get to know each other. Plus, sexual temptation is higher when a couple lacks the protection that naturally comes from being in group settings. And since the goal of unselfish dating is to determine whether the couple should proceed toward marriage, input from loving family and friends who see how they relate to one another can be invaluable.

Another way Rebecca stays under the protection of others is by having a mentor to talk over tough stuff she may not feel comfortable discussing with other older people in her life. Rebecca feels that the Lord led her to her mentor, a middle-aged woman who speaks into her life often. Because they live in different states, they usually discuss what's going on in Rebecca's life and pray together over the phone rather than in person. Rebecca also considers her grandmother to be one of her mentors. Since her grandfather's death nearly a decade ago, Rebecca and her grandma have taken many trips together. Rebecca likes to spend time with her grandmother and wants to be influenced by her.

THREE IMPORTANT QUESTIONS

To determine whether something is right or wrong in a romantic relationship—like the ever popular "how far is too far" question—Rebecca asks herself three questions:

1. Is God happy with what I'm doing right now, or does He consider this relationship impure?
2. Would I have a hard time explaining this to my future husband if *this guy* isn't him?
3. Would I have a hard time explaining these actions to my future kids?

In her book *Wait for Me,* Rebecca further explains these three questions. She wants every area of her life to bring glory to God and is committed to honoring her future husband *now*—even before she knows who he is. "One of the gifts I can already be preparing for my future kids is my purity—showing them that I loved and respected their father by being faithful to him before I'd even met him."[7]

Rebecca does not believe, however, that all physical interaction in a romantic relationship is wrong or would dishonor her future husband if she does not end up marrying that person. Rebecca explains how she keeps her commitment to purity while being in the stage of a romantic relationship that is prior to being engaged or married:

> I am not of the school that discourages any physical interaction whatsoever (unless God has specifically given you that personal conviction). In my own experience you can have a certain amount of limited physical affection (hand-holding, arm around the shoulder, etc.), and through it you can actually experience God's love and joy. Our loving Father has given us the ability to enjoy one another's presence, and part of that joy is expressed through physical touch—done in a godly way! But be very careful that what is going on in your actions and in your thoughts is pure. If you have a prior experience of falling in the physical area, be very cautious, set up and stick to your boundaries, and don't put yourself in vulnerable situations.[8]

Because of Rebecca's personal convictions and public platform on purity, a guy has to be a Christian—and a strong one at that—before she will consider dating him. For one thing, very early in the relationship she tells the guy what physical boundaries she has in place to make sure there is no room for sexual compromise. Being up front about her standards of integrity does two things:

- ⌒ It weeds out anyone who doesn't welcome having a relationship with her within those boundaries.
- ⌒ The guy doesn't get his feelings hurt by thinking that she is rejecting him when he begins to express his affection in a way that would be okay with a lot of other girls but would cross a line for Rebecca.

At this point you might be wondering if there really are guys out there who are sold out and committed to purity. Rebecca told me that just about the time she starts to feel discouraged, she'll meet a godly young man who is wholeheartedly sold out to God and committed to purity.

Recently, she was encouraged by a guy who came up to talk to her after one of her concerts. When he told her that he thought her commitment to purity was awesome, Rebecca felt like it was a little reminder from God that there really are guys out there who feel the same way she does. In fact, when he told her that most girls he meets don't seem interested in being in a relationship with a guy who is committed to keeping his life pure before God, she realized that their meeting was actually an encouragement to both of them.

> "This guy told me that a lot of times he gets the feeling that girls don't even want a guy who is committed to purity."

But Rebecca (and probably you!) has found that not all guys are as sold out to God as that guy seemed to be. She's noticed that all too often girls are the ones who end up carrying the responsibility of maintaining sexual purity in a relationship. This has sometimes been the case in her own dating relationships, which has left her feeling disappointed because the guy didn't take the lead when it came to purity.

And Rebecca doesn't buy into the idea that the way guys are made gives them an excuse for being led around by their sexual desires—as if their defense is simply that it's "biological." She also gets offended when people come up to her after a concert and thank her for talking to *the girls* about sexual purity. "I feel like grabbing their arm and saying, 'HELLO, I'm not just talking to the girls. I'm talking to both guys and girls.'" The same week Rebecca and I talked, she had a chance to set the record straight on this when a journalist who was interviewing her began to imply that purity is only the girl's responsibility. Rebecca quickly jumped in and said, "You know what? This issue is not just for girls. It's important for both girls *and* guys to be committed to purity."

THE ROMANCE OF WAITING UNTIL MARRIAGE

Rebecca told me straight up and without hesitation that she has never been in a situation where she has been tempted to actually have sex. That's right—*never.* So given the sexually motivated culture we live in, how is that possible for someone in her midtwenties? According to Rebecca, it's because she *always* stays well within the boundaries she has in place for herself—which we now know about too!

Does Rebecca want to get married? Yes! But she also sees the blessings of being single. Like being able to focus on God and the calling He has for her right now and to devote more time to relationships with family and friends.

Dreaming of Him

The blessing of purity is God's perfect plan for our lives, a plan that is intended to bring us joy and maximum fulfillment—instead of pain and disappointment.

If we live in obedience to God's call for purity, there is no sin-barrier to keep God's favor, blessing, and presence from saturating our lives. Plus, being set apart in purity until marriage paves the way for God to ultimately bless our physical expressions of love to our marriage partner in a splendid way.

Imagine for a moment your wedding night. Imagine your honeymoon night—that you and your new husband have both reserved that precious gift of intimacy, which you will now give to each

Pure intimacy…pure romance…is worth waiting for and fighting for.

other. Neither of you has any preconceived expectations of what this experience should be like. No old tapes of past sexual experiences are playing in your heads, distracting or hindering your free expression of love for each other. Neither of you has anyone else's body or lovemaking to compare each other to.

You have waited—and *fought*—for this pure intimacy, this pure romance, this virgin love. All you know of physical intimacy is what you are about to experience together.

Rebecca believes that the day will come when she will marry. She holds the promise she feels God has given her close to her heart—that at some time in her life He will provide her with a husband.

And while she waits for her husband, she dreams of *him waiting for her.* Her dream of him helps her guard her purity. She even writes love letters to him, dreaming of the pure romance that awaits them, dreaming of the day when they will meet and then complete their journey together toward marriage, dreaming of the day when she will give him the treasure of letters she has written to him over the years as she has waited for and dreamed of…him.

Beauty Inside Out

meghanrowe

There is no doubt that the Bible's Esther could turn heads with her physical appearance. This young lady was naturally stunning, described as "lovely in form and features" (Esther 2:7). She certainly wouldn't have attracted the attention of the king's commissioners if she hadn't possessed an outer beauty.

Yet Esther's other qualities—her *inner* beauty—were what ultimately set her apart. She won the favor and approval of Hegai, and eventually the king himself, because she was the whole package. Esther was attractive, certainly, but also so much more—obedient, reverent, faithful, courageous. This was a young woman with plenty to offer.

Many young women today, on the other hand, feel they have very little to offer. Maybe you're one of them. Maybe without even realizing it, you've bought into the lies our culture promotes: that image is everything, appearance is what matters, and if you aren't gorgeous, you're a nobody.

Meghan Rowe can relate.

ELEPHANT MAN

Meghan grew up with all the usual girl problems—plus one more. She suffers from neurofibromatosis (NF), a progressive genetic disorder that can lead to a wide range of serious health issues: tumors, skin changes, bone deformities, disfigurement, blindness, deafness, loss of limbs, and learning disabilities.

Fortunately, Meghan's NF hasn't been too severe so far. She did have a tumor surgically removed from her spine when she was eight years old and has also undergone surgeries on her feet. Other than a few small growths on her face, her condition wasn't immediately obvious to others—but when classmates found out about it, they teased Meghan mercilessly, calling her "Elephant Man" and other humiliating names.

Holding on to self-esteem through childhood is tough for any girl, but for Meghan it was a losing battle. She felt abnormal and angry.

"I just thought it was really unfair," she remembers. "I hadn't done anything to deserve this, so why was it happening to me? I had to go to the doctors all the time for CAT scans, MRIs, things like that, and the surgeries were really painful. I was angry that I wasn't like all the other kids."

A NEW PERSPECTIVE

The anger began to melt away when Meghan was fourteen. She had been raised in a Catholic family, but that summer a counselor named Michele introduced her to a personal relationship with Jesus. Slowly Meghan's perspective began to change, though she still didn't understand why God was allowing this condition in her life.

Meghan had accepted Christ as a young teen, but it wasn't until she was in her twenties that her faith really began to grow. Along with that growth came new insights—such as a realization that true beauty has nothing to do with physical appearance.

"God is showing me that real beauty comes from the inside, from the heart," Meghan told me recently. "You can be the most physically beautiful person on the face of the planet, but if you don't have that inner beauty, it doesn't really matter. Our physical bodies are just temporary, anyway. Our spirit is what's going to last."

Meghan has also begun to see that, just as He did with Esther, God might in fact be preparing her for a time and purpose bigger than herself.

"I know now that God doesn't give us what we can't handle, that He *does* have a reason for what He does," Meghan says. "He chose me because He can use me. I think He allowed me to have NF because I can help other people that have it. I know what it's like to have grown up with it—to have been teased and ostracized because of it—and I think that's made me compassionate toward other people who might be experiencing the same thing. God has given me a heart to help people."

This bittersweet experience of living with physical deformity has given Meghan an inner beauty she might not otherwise have had. Many times it is the challenges we face in life that develop inner beauty like compassion, humility, perspective, and grace. Meghan has allowed this painful experience to work God's character in her, and that is very attractive on a girl.

THE REAL MEGHAN

Let's be honest—most of us fantasize about changing our appearance at one time or another. Haven't you ever wished for the perfect body or perfect skin, or wondered what you might look like with blue eyes instead of brown? Maybe you've already switched your hair color from brown to blond (or purple?).

It's easy, especially in today's image-crazed society, to obsess over appearances. But I think God has more important plans for the way we invest our thoughts and time. He wants us to check out our *inner* selves, the gifts and heart passions that He's planted in us. I believe nothing would please God more than for us to go to Him and ask how He wants us to use those gifts and desires.

That's what Meghan is doing. More and more, she has been seeking—and finding—answers to how God wants to use her passion for helping people. For instance, when she heard that there was going to be a half marathon in her hometown of Virginia Beach to raise funds for NF research, she called and offered to work as a volunteer. But after thinking about it and doing a few training runs, she decided to register and quietly run in the race herself. Then came a call from the race organizers: Would she be willing to sign up sponsors and raise money too? Meghan found herself saying yes.

The process of raising awareness and funds wasn't easy for Meghan, however. For years she'd hidden her condition from friends, fearing that they would reject her or treat her differently if they knew about it. When the time came to "go public," with an e-mail message about what she was doing, she struggled.

"I agonized over sending that e-mail," Meghan says. "There was that fear of telling everybody about it because of my experiences when I was younger. It probably took me a good half hour before I could hit the 'send' button. But when I did and I started getting responses back, it was just overwhelming how supportive everybody was."

Meghan found a new freedom in revealing herself to her friends and greater purpose as she increased NF awareness in the community and raised money for research. She also finished all thirteen-plus miles of the race despite a training injury (way to go, girl!). Yet those are not the only ways she is answering God's call on her life.

GOD'S PRINCESS

A former pianist and occasional guitar player, Meghan now sings with the worship team at her church. She is meeting with two small women's groups and seeing incredible opportunities to support and be blessed by caring Christian friends.

Meghan is also very active in ORPHANetwork, a nonprofit organization dedicated to helping orphans in Nicaragua and the Ukraine. She recently completed her first missions trip, a weeklong visit to a Nicaraguan orphanage. She describes her experience with the network as "a blessing to see what they are doing in children's lives. It's been a real blessing to me as well."

What I find a blessing is to hear how Meghan has begun to measure her value in terms of what God sees, rather than what the world sees. Like Esther, Meghan is a young woman of royalty—a princess in God's court.

"I never used to think of myself as being a princess," she says, "but you know, God is king and we're all His kids, so that really is what we are. He gives each of us gifts, and I'm learning to recognize what those gifts are and how to put them into practice."

Meghan is so grateful that God is deepening her faith and opening her eyes to the purposes He has for her life. She wants to encourage modern-day Esthers—young women like you—to discover their own true value and gifts and to choose to live out a radical faith.

"It's really a matter of going against the flow," she says. "Society wants you to be more concerned about having the right hair, having the right clothes, having the right boyfriend, having the right car, and life isn't about that. Yeah, you might lose friends if you're not going to parties and drinking or not having sex with your boyfriend or things like that. But I think it's important for people to notice something different about you, and that 'something different' will be God working through you. If you're truly trying to follow Him, He's going to bless your life in ways you can't even imagine."

BEAUTY FROM WITHIN

God is blessing Meghan today, working through her in noticeable ways. Her inner beauty is shining through. Her life reflects the words of the apostle Peter: "You should be known for the beauty that comes from within, the unfading beauty of a gentle and quiet spirit, which is so precious to God" (1 Peter 3:4, NLT).

Did you catch that word? *Precious.* That's how God views inner beauty. It's also what He thinks of you. He sees right through your outer appearance and into the beautiful, *real* you on the inside, the one He imagined and designed before you were born. As you spend more and more time cultivating an intimate relationship with the Lord, He will reveal the gifts He's given you and the plans He's made for you.

Like Meghan and Esther, you too will discover a life of beauty—from the inside out.

chapter five

Choosing to Be Set Apart

lisa bevere

During Lisa Bevere's first three years at the University of Arizona, walking from one class to another was a big social event, running into friends, chatting about her latest crush or last night's party. During her sophomore year alone, Lisa dated a whopping forty-five guys—and she loved to brag about it. But actually, all this male attention had come as a bit of a shock to Lisa....

From the age of five, Lisa Bevere had come to expect the kind of rejection that included being called names like "Cyclops." You see, doctors had been forced to remove Lisa's right eye after discovering that she had cancer in her eye and had perhaps only six months to live if they didn't take drastic action. When Lisa went back to school, she had to wear a patch over the area where her eye had once been. The kids made fun of her, and she thought she looked like a pirate. Soon this little five-year-old felt incredibly ugly, distorted, and unnatural.

At the end of a school day, as soon as the bell rang, Lisa would run home and cry in her mother's lap. Why had God let her lose her eye? Why had He let her have cancer? Why couldn't she be like the other girls? Why did she have to be so different? With each passing day, Lisa's anger about her situation grew. She even felt resentful toward God because of the cancer.

HIDING THE DIFFERENCE

The tormenting Lisa endured at school continued—even after being fitted with an artificial eye. At that time, artificial eyes were quite obvious. The eye stuck out, and the kids continued to call her names, like One-Eye and Cyclops. "I felt like a giant artificial-eye-with-legs walking down the hallways at school," Lisa told me.

Sometimes guys taunted her by telling her she would've been one of the prettiest girls in the school if she hadn't lost her eye. Their backhanded compliments made her feel even worse about herself. "I was like, 'Okay, that was supposed to make me feel good?'"

With each passing day, Lisa's anger about her situation grew.

She tried to hide the abnormality by parting her hair on the left; however, sweeping her hair over the artificial eye only drew more attention to it. Hunching her shoulders and turning her head to the right didn't hide the prosthesis either.

When school pictures were taken, Lisa was petrified of how hers would look. The stress was almost unbearable right up until the day the pictures were handed out. As Lisa scanned her photo, she could see only one thing: the eye, the gargantuan plastic eye, bulging out and declaring her horribly different from all the other kids.

TOUGH GIRLS DON'T GET HURT

Along with all this, Lisa's dad pretty much ignored her after her eye was taken out. When he did pay attention to her, he referred to her as "Tiger" or "Little Scrapper" and told her that he was proud of how she was toughing it out like a champ. While still in elementary school, Lisa began hiding her wounded heart behind a "tough girl" image, which helped shield her from being hurt by the nicknames the kids at school called her.

At first, being rough and tough was a way of acting out some of the anger she had built up toward God and toward the people who had rejected her. But then, in the fifth grade, Lisa watched a James Bond movie and saw a different kind of tough girl: the tough and seductive Bond woman who wore hot pants and packed a gun, never got hurt, was in control, and always got her man—at least for one night. Lisa became convinced that this was an image she could hide behind, a way she could feel safe.

She quickly discovered the power that came with dressing seductively. During a pep rally where she was supposed to sing a line in a skit from the song "California Girls," she decided that the best way to mask her fear of standing in front of the whole student body was to dress like a Bond babe. The boys in the bleachers went wild when Lisa walked into the auditorium wearing her mom's knee-high leather boots, some black hot pants, and a tight sweater while singing, "And the northern girls with the way they kiss, they keep their boyfriends warm at night." Although Lisa soon faded back into obscurity after that incident, she had come to realize that being a tough girl gave her power.

SUDDENLY IN DEMAND

When Lisa left her hometown in Indiana to go to college in sunny Arizona, one guy after another flirted with her and asked her out. She actually began to *enjoy* being sexually attractive to guys. She particularly loved stringing guys along and then dropping them before they had a chance to discover the secret she hoped to keep tucked away in her former life in Indiana—that deep down she wasn't really *cool* or *in control*.

These guys didn't give her artificial eye a second thought. But since Lisa still felt like a loser, she would drop a guy the minute she started feeling close to him. She was determined not to take any chances that one of the thirty-seven thousand students at the university would find out she really wasn't "all that" after all.

Another manifestation of Lisa's insecurity about her looks was that she became obsessed with her weight. With this obsession came anorexia. She starved herself and took laxatives and diuretics—it was a battle that lasted for years.

Although she was insecure on the inside, Lisa continued to pursue popularity. She rushed a sorority just prior to her freshman year and quickly earned the reputation of a party girl. She ran with a wild crowd and by age nineteen had lost her virginity to a twenty-seven-year-old man who hit on freshman girls at nightspots where students hung out. Over several months he had worn down her resolve, until finally she gave in fully to his seductions. She returned home for the summer to escape the hold this man had on her.

Even though Lisa had tried hard to control everything—her social status, her surroundings, her impression on others—her life seemed to be spinning out of control.

A SHOCKING DIFFERENCE

But then everything changed. Over the summer between Lisa's junior and senior years of college, she heard for the first time how much God loved and desired her. Overwhelmed by a love so unconditional, Lisa surrendered her life to Christ and became a new person. John, the young man who had taken the time to share God's love with Lisa, was very different from all the guys Lisa had known before, and he would eventually become her husband.

And when she returned to college her senior year, her sorority sisters noticed right away that something about her was different. As soon as she walked through the door of her sorority house, she was bombarded with questions: "Why do you look so great?" "Have you lost weight?" "Did you cut your hair?"

"No…" Lisa answered. "But I did become a Christian while I was back home."

This statement was met with groans, rolling eyes, and yawns. It seemed obvious to Lisa that her sorority sisters wanted to get out of this conversation as quickly as possible, but Lisa felt it was important to give Jesus the credit for her happiness and the changes her sisters could see in her.

"I used to have total death, but now I have total life," Lisa told them. "And I'm not struggling with my eating disorder anymore. God even healed the damage I did to my stomach." The change Christ had made in Lisa's life was real. Her healing and new outlook on life were a testimony to God's healing power.

To learn more about how Lisa Bevere overcame her eating disorder and came to understand more about God's love for her, check out her book "You Are Not What You Weigh."

A DIFFERENT KIND OF REJECTION

Lisa was a different person now. And as her senior year got underway, most of her partying friends didn't try to hide the fact that they had liked her much better drunk, wild, and running around with one guy after another. She just wasn't as much "fun" as she used to be. Girls who had formerly been friends would get up and walk away when she sat with them at lunch. Lisa was reminded all over again of those years she was ignored or called names by the kids at school.

But this was different. The rejection Lisa had experienced when she was younger was because of a difference that was beyond her control— her artificial eye. Now she was being rejected because she was *choosing* to be different. With her conversion had come the decision to be set apart. Not only did she want to be different from non-Christians; she also wanted to be different from her sorority sisters who carefully hid the fact that they considered themselves Christians. How was it possible that she had known these girls for three years and just now was learning that they were Christians?

Living out her new faith was hard at first. Lisa bent under the pressure not to be radically different—that is, to be so different that she turned off non-Christians to the whole idea of Christianity. She even went to some parties just to prove that a person can be a Christian and still be "cool." But now that she wasn't getting drunk, the whole party scene seemed ridiculous. As Lisa, a very new and uncertain Christian, tried to figure out what was okay and what wasn't, she had no idea that she would soon be faced with a moment of decision—when she would either hide behind a mask in order to avoid humiliation or rise to the call to be set apart for God.

JUMPING FOR JESUS

Lisa was taken totally by surprise when her moment of destiny arose the very first week she was back at school. It seemed like any other day as she sat in class with the other students, waiting for the professor to enter the large lecture hall. Suddenly Lisa's name was yelled out loudly enough for all two hundred students in the room to hear.

Her heart skipped a beat.

The student body president called out from the front row, "Hey, Lisa! Is it true what I hear? Are you jumping for Jesus? Well, we won't stand for it! We will kidnap you from the Theta house and make you join us in sex, drugs, and alcohol!"[1]

Lisa was at a crossroad—she could either stand up for her faith or shrink back in fear.

Was this really happening? Lisa's heart began pounding so hard that it felt like it was going to jump right out of her chest. "I was absolutely terrified. I'd like to say that I had a real peace and felt like this was really exciting. But the challenge came when I didn't expect it. It definitely came in a setting that was outside my control. I thought, *Surely God doesn't want me to be embarrassed.*"

But Lisa recognized that this was an opportunity for her to publicly proclaim her faith. This was *her* Esther moment—that "Aha"…"Oh no" moment—when she would be forced to make a decision. Would she embrace her faith and share it with others, which might cost her her reputation? Or would she hide behind her fear?

Lisa saw that everyone in the room was either looking at her or trying to figure out who the student body president was talking to. She felt a wave of terror and shame crash over her. Some people were even laughing and nodding in her direction.

In the moment before she responded to the president's challenge, her mind raced. Lisa was at a crossroad.

Wouldn't it be easier for everyone if she just hunched down in her chair and went along with the voice of compromise that was whispering in her head, *You don't want him to think that Christians don't have fun, do you? Come on now, you don't want him to think that a person has to be really sold out to God.... You can be a Christian and have the world too.*

But Lisa didn't want to be a closet Christian. Just that week she had asked several girls in her sorority, "So, if you've been Christians all these years we've been friends, why didn't I know it?" Lisa knew she wanted to be more sold out to being a Christian than she had been to being a heathen. As Lisa weighed how to respond, a Scripture popped into her head:

> "Whoever acknowledges me before men, I will also acknowledge him before my Father in heaven. But whoever disowns me before men, I will disown him before my Father in heaven."
>
> MATTHEW 10:32–33

Although she had been a Christian for only six weeks, Lisa recognized that the Spirit of the Lord was nudging her by bringing this Scripture to her mind. Before she had time even to give her predicament another thought, she suddenly realized that she was standing. And two hundred pairs of eyes were fixed on her, waiting for her response.

This was it. This was her moment to set herself apart for the Lord. Lisa looked squarely into the student body president's eyes and announced calmly, "It's true." And with that declaration, she jumped up and down to make sure they knew she meant it.

The president, and nearly everyone else, roared with laughter. She sat back down, not nearly as calm and collected as she might've seemed when she literally "jumped for Jesus." In fact, her trembling on the inside had turned into shaking on the outside. From the time the professor walked in until the moment the class ended that day, Lisa stared straight ahead, waiting for her chance to escape the auditorium.

OTHERS ARE WATCHING

Lisa wasn't sure the episode in class that day had done much to inspire others to jump for Jesus, but she knew that she was now accountable to the many people who would be watching to see if her life matched the bold statement she had made. "I didn't feel like I had done something incredibly empowering, but I knew that I had gone out and positioned myself where I needed to be."

Lisa recognized that she would be challenged again and again by kids on campus, who would either mock her or try to sway her from her stand in Christ. In fact, much of the confrontation would probably come from the people she had been friends with. Rather than slinking back into obscurity, which would've been easier, Lisa decided that she would always be ready to defend her love for the Lord.

> Through thick and thin, keep your hearts at attention, in adoration before Christ, your Master. Be ready to speak up and tell anyone who asks why you're living the way you are, and always with the utmost courtesy.
>
> I PETER 3:15, *THE MESSAGE*

People would be watching Lisa, waiting to see how she would live now as a Christian, so she decided to use this to her advantage. She looked at those people as a big accountability group. Many people on campus knew Lisa as a wild partier; now she wanted to be known as a Christian woman who was set apart for God and His purposes.

As for the student body president, he never challenged Lisa again. After seeing that she was so committed to standing strong in Christ that she would actually humiliate herself if need be, he completely backed off.

That semester certainly wasn't easy for Lisa. She spent most of it alone and felt quite isolated. God and His Word were often her only companions. "At first I didn't understand what God was doing. I kept asking, *Why am I being isolated?*" Lisa began to see God's purposes for her more clearly as she became immersed in the book of Esther. "We can view the preparation time of God as our time of isolation from man. Esther was isolated, and yet it was not because of rejection, but for preparation.

"God began to tell me that He had set me apart for Him, not for ministry. He wanted every area of my life. It wasn't 'I'm saved…now I'm done.' God was saying, 'Now that you're saved, I want to set you apart. I want to sanctify you unto Me. I want you to separate every area of your life to My keeping.'"

Lisa desperately wanted the kinds of maiden friends she had read about in the book of Esther, but didn't have any strong Christian friends on campus. In fact, two of her few Christian girlfriends became pregnant outside of marriage, which wasn't a good influence for such a new Christian just learning how to live God's way. Although she didn't have close maiden friends during that time of growth, God placed within Lisa a desire for that, which would be filled later in her life.

As Lisa walked the campus, people often gave her looks that seemed to say, "We know who you really are. It won't be long before you join us again," or "Come on. Haven't you had enough of this God stuff? Isn't it about time you came back with us?" Lisa's social life was a huge part of who she was. In the past, her social status had defined her. But now she was alone. "Over those years I had chosen the wrong men. I had chosen the wrong friends. My friendships had been developed during the years when I was a party girl." Lisa says, "It was my biggest idol, and it had to be killed."

Lisa did date a bit that semester. She even tried to witness and study the Bible with guys she had been intimate with before. But that didn't last long. She quickly saw that she had to completely cut herself off from them. Despite her attempts to separate herself from her emotional attachments to these guys, they were so entangled that she asked the Lord to sever those ties that she alone could not cut. Lisa also decided to separate herself from movies, music, books, and surroundings that might awaken the unwholesome thoughts and emotions that had once controlled her.

DISCOVERING TRUE STRENGTH

Esther was the first book of the Bible God led Lisa to read. As she read the chapters over and over, she realized that she too had been born "for such a time as this."

For years, Lisa had hidden her fears and insecurities behind a number of different images. But reading about Esther helped Lisa understand that true courage and godly influence would be hers only after she submitted all aspects of her life to the Lord. Meditating on how Esther refused to give in to fear and walked in authority because she was submitted to authority helped Lisa understand that true strength can be found only in identifying the ways God gives people favor so they can help others. In Esther, Lisa saw the beauty of being truly set apart for the Lord.

Lisa transferred to another school at the end of that fall semester. Shortly after transferring, she began dating John Bevere, whom she had been dating during that wondrous summer when she became a Christian. John was the person who had led her to the gift of salvation, which is available only through belief in the Lord Jesus Christ. He was also the man who would become her husband, her companion in ministry, and the father of her four sons.

POSITIONED TO HELP OTHER GIRLS

Now a popular speaker and author of numerous books, Lisa is committed to helping young women avoid the pain of living a life that is not set apart. "I believe that every generation has a mandate on it to pass on truth to the next generation, whether those are truths we have lived or truths we have painfully learned by not living them. I don't want the next generation to have the same kind of regret I have known." She encourages women to let sexual desires remain dormant until they are married. Lisa is passionate about supporting and equipping young women to rise up into God's call for them to be modern-day Esthers.

With all she has learned, what would Lisa say to young women today? When I asked her this, she responded by quoting from Isaiah 52: "Awake, awake, O Zion, clothe yourself with strength" (v. 1).

"I would give young women a charge," Lisa said, "that there is a cry in the Spirit that they must 'awake' and step into the dream God has put on each of their lives. When they begin to move into that, they will find the garments of shame falling off and the splendor He has waiting for them."

Lisa prays that today's Esthers will be so set apart that everyone who looks upon them will know that they are God's.

Lisa Bevere's bestselling book "Kissed the Girls and Made Them Cry" is a must-read to help you discover more ways to rise up into the fullness of God's call upon your life.

chapter six

Unlikely Esthers Positioned in a World Crisis

heathermercer & daynacurry

The horrifying events of what we have now come to call "9/11" are forever burned in the minds of all Americans. News that two jumbo jets had crashed into the Twin Towers of the World Trade Center in New York City, sending them crumbling to the earth, as well as the other terrorist acts that day, stunned the nation. As events unfolded, much of the focus in America was on trying to understand how this could have happened, what it all meant, and what was to come.

Thousands of miles away, in a country called home to the terrorist organization behind the attacks, two young American women sat in a dark, dingy room pondering similar questions. These girls were virtually unknown until news reports began to reveal their plight and apparent fate—death.

Dayna Curry and Heather Mercer, two young missionaries in Afghanistan, had been arrested on August 3, 2001, for allegedly trying to convert Muslims to Christianity. On September 8—just three days before the tragedy of 9/11—the supreme court of Afghanistan seemed to imply that they were facing a possible death sentence, which could be carried out by stoning, firing squad, or being buried alive. When the news of 9/11 reached Heather and Dayna, a prison guard told them, "You will be fine if America does not attack Afghanistan. But if America attacks, it will be very bad for you."[1] As American news media began to focus on their captivity, it became clear that Heather and Dayna were now pawns in an international conflict.

Much like Esther, these girls faced death because their beliefs contradicted the culture around them. But these modern-day Esthers would soon realize that God had positioned them as spiritual warriors with a unique destiny. And though death looked increasingly likely, their hope was alive and was touching the lives of the people in this hostile land. Heather and Dayna's story is one of unlikely Esthers coming face-to-face with an unimaginable destiny.

OBEDIENT TO THE CALL

Before I explain why Heather and Dayna were unlikely Esthers, it's important to understand what exactly these young American women were doing half a world away in Afghanistan. What had they done to deserve a death sentence? And where was God in the midst of this crisis?

Years before, a passion for sharing God's love with the Afghan people had stirred in both Dayna and Heather when they heard a humanitarian aid worker tell of the people's critical needs. Their compassion for the Afghan people grew deeper when they began to pray regularly for Afghanistan. Motivated by a need to act on their prayers, each girl took short-term trips to Afghanistan and saw firsthand the devastation in the country and the suffering of the people—especially the women.

For example, the strict Taliban laws were constantly changing, which meant Afghans lived in constant fear of being beaten, tortured, imprisoned, or even killed for breaking some new law they didn't even know existed. An Afghan woman might be beaten for wearing nail polish or for not wearing socks with her shoes. Or she might be imprisoned for speaking to a man that was not her husband or a close male relative. Often, girls as young as twelve were put in prison for running away from their abusive middle-aged husbands or husbands-to-be.

Finally, Heather and Dayna were compelled to make the ultimate commitment. Only in their twenties, they decided to give up the security and comfort of home in Waco, Texas, to journey to a war-torn country ruled by Islamic extremists. With few personal belongings in hand, they made their way to what would be their new home, in Kabul. They had no idea what awaited them—or how their lives were about to change.

Bullet holes in the wall enclosing their backyard were constant reminders that war could be just around the corner.

Sixty to seventy percent of the buildings in Kabul had been bombed out during the twenty-plus years of war that had raged in Afghanistan. The small concrete building that became their home was once a storehouse for weapons and ammunition. The inside had been remodeled, but bullet holes in the wall enclosing their backyard were constant reminders that war could be just around the corner.

Rather than focusing on all the dangers of living in a city that was a hub for terrorist activity, the girls turned their attention to the needs of the people. The Afghan neighborhood called Wazir Akhbar Khan would provide plenty of opportunities to get to know people and help them in small ways.

Right away, Dayna and Heather wanted to get to know the Afghan women, especially those hidden beneath the garments—called *burqas*—they were required to wear, which covered them completely from head to toe. The only opening was a small slit for their eyes. The girls began organizing the crowds of poor Afghan women who gathered at their gate during the day to ask for food, money, medicine, and work. A Talib had viciously beaten a group of Afghan women for standing outside a house where other Westerners lived, so Heather and Dayna responded quickly when one of their Talib neighbors complained—they arranged for the women and children to come only at scheduled times.

Had they tried to convince any Muslims to become Christians?

While trying to relieve some of the physical suffering around them, Heather and Dayna also tried to find ways to touch the people's spiritual hunger. Sometimes this involved sharing how Christ had changed their lives; sometimes simply praying quietly with a desperate woman was all they could do. TVs and movies were banned, but the organization they were associated with was able to use a laptop computer to show the movie *The Jesus Film*. Because of the danger of being caught, this was usually done in extreme secret in a host's home.

Heather and Dayna went to a home one day to show the film to a family they had visited several times. The family was curious about Jesus and wanted to see the film. In the past, Dayna's laptop had been used to show the film, but on this day the CD wasn't working and the audio wasn't loud enough for the large group of extended family that had come. Frustrated and a bit anxious, they finally got it running.

Heather stayed with the family as the movie played, but Dayna took a taxi to meet a friend. Suddenly, her taxi stopped. Armed Talib police climbed into the taxi and whisked her away. Shortly after that, another group of men arrested Heather at a different location and took her to the Vice and Virtue Building, where Dayna was being held for interrogation. Suddenly, their world had changed…again!

LADIES-IN-WAITING

During the first few weeks after their arrest, Heather and Dayna were treated fairly and believed the Taliban authorities' assurances that they would be released very soon. Each time they were questioned, their interrogators tried to mislead them into thinking that how they answered the questions was not a serious matter. However, Dayna and Heather knew that giving their interrogators certain kinds of information could have deadly consequences for them and for the families they had befriended. Questions to be answered very cautiously included:

- Had they tried to convince any Muslims to become Christians?
- Had they shown a film about Jesus to Afghans?
- Had they given books about Jesus to Afghans?

Dayna and Heather had been arrested with four other women from the German-based foreign aid group Shelter Now International (SNI). As days turned into weeks, the women spent their time in captivity praying, singing praise and worship songs, and reading their Bibles.

They also looked for ways to help the Afghan women imprisoned at the same compound. For example, because Dayna and Heather and the other foreigners had money and the favor of the guards, they could have items delivered to them from the local marketplace or from the American Embassy. The Afghan women, on the other hand, did not have this kind of access. To help them, Dayna and Heather would often slip treats or necessities to them. Sometimes they would

At night they often heard the screams of Afghan prisoners, both men and women, being beaten or tortured.

try to brighten the women's days by doing little things like sneaking M&M candies to them. Other times they tried to relieve their suffering in small ways— like slipping aspirin to a girl who had been severely beaten by the guards, or using lice shampoo sent from the American Embassy to wash the women's lice-infested hair.

At night they often heard the screams of Afghan prisoners, both men and women, being beaten or tortured. They tearfully cried out to God on behalf of these people, who were often falsely accused or being beaten for the smallest offense. They prayed for the nation of Afghanistan to be released from captivity and suffering and for the world to become aware of their oppression.

MESSAGES FROM MORDECAI

Two men from their group, Georg and Peter, were imprisoned in another part of the compound. Georg, the organization's leader in Kabul before the arrests, continued to encourage the women even after they were put in prison. In somewhat the same way as Mordecai communicated with Esther through one of the king's eunuchs (see Esther 4), Georg sent notes to the women through a guard who treated them with kindness.

One day Georg encouraged them to read the book of Esther. Dayna read the whole book in one sitting and was strengthened deep within her heart as she compared Esther's situation to her own. Perhaps *this* situation was their "for such a time as this."

FAITH VERSUS FEAR

About a month after their arrest, Heather and Dayna were taken before the Afghan Supreme Court. Under a Taliban ruling issued in January 2001, any Afghan Muslim who converted to another religion would be sentenced to death. Some reports suggested that any foreigner who shared a non-Muslim faith with an Afghan would also be sentenced to death.

When Dayna and Heather moved to Kabul, they knew that their safety was at risk. They had considered the fact that they might die. But at some point during their imprisonment, each of them came to a place of *fully* surrendering her life to the Lord—becoming truly willing to die.

For Dayna, this happened when British journalist Yvonne Ridley was imprisoned with them for several days and told them the horrifying details of the 9/11 disaster. The eight prisoners were overcome with sorrow. She went on to tell them that Mullah Mohammad Omar, the supreme ruler of the Taliban, had proposed a trade-off to President George W. Bush: Eight aid workers would go free if the American government agreed not to bomb Afghanistan. But Yvonne was not optimistic: "It's not a matter of if the U.S. will bomb, but when. You must brace yourselves for it."[2]

That night, Dayna recalled the story of Esther. She had her own Esther moment:

I was awake in my bed for hours that night; my heart physically hurt. We had spent a lot of time praying for the American families who lost loved ones back when we first found out about the tragedy, but now we felt the impact of the events in a profound way. How could we dare to hope the President would hold off bombing for the eight of us when so many had died? Action needed to be taken against Osama bin Laden. *Our lives were in God's hands. If we perished, we perished.*[3]

ITALICS MINE

Over time, as bits of news from the outside world reached them, they began to realize that they were in a unique position to do things they couldn't have done if they hadn't been arrested and imprisoned. Perhaps like Esther, they were being providentially positioned in the midst of a crisis for a divine purpose...for such a time as this.

- As they worshiped and prayed in that Islamic fortress, the name of Jesus was being lifted up in a place where it had never been exalted before.

- Because the other foreign aid workers had been forced to flee, they were the only Christians praying from inside Kabul.

- Because they shared a courtyard with the Afghan women imprisoned there, they were able to observe firsthand the women's suffering, pray for them, dance and sing with them, tell them about Jesus, and help with some of their critical needs.

- While being questioned, they were able to tell Islamic officials and guards about the love of Jesus Christ.

- Because the media had spread the news of their imprisonment, Christians around the world suddenly started praying fervently for Afghanistan.

- Their own faith was challenged like never before *and* was growing like never before. And there was great comfort in knowing they were joining with all those who had gone before them and suffered for the cause of Christ.

On October 7, the U.S. started bombing Taliban strongholds. At times, the bombs struck so close to the prison that the building shook and the interior doors blew open. For weeks, Heather barricaded herself under a cot while bombs were dropped night after night. When the bombs began to be dropped around the clock, she became so emotionally exhausted that she didn't know how much longer she could go on. Finally, too exhausted to wrestle any longer with her possible death, Heather came to the point of fully surrendering to the Lord. She wrote in her journal:

> Lord, all I can do is throw myself in Your hands and say, "Have Your way." I am utterly desperate and I can do nothing, so I put my life in Your hands. By now I've gone numb. It's as though I can't take any more, so I just have to shut down. God, I trust You! Lord, You're my only hope. I resign now and ask for Your grace to endure… Oh God, I want to live, but my life is in Your hands. *If I live, I live for You. If I die, I die for You.* In the end, You are in control and You have the last word.[4]

ITALICS MINE

Heather's Esther moment was both freeing and empowering. Just hours before they were forced to flee the city with the Taliban—and moments before Kabul fell into the hands of the Northern Alliance—Heather read Scriptures to the weary group and led them in singing the songs they had made up during their time there. Seated atop rocket launchers, they had no idea where they were being taken, but they were leaving the prison singing, just as they had prayed they would.

If I live, I live for You. If I die, I die for You.

Dayna noted that it was Heather who took the lead during the time when their future was most uncertain:

[Heather] pulled out her flashlight and began to read to us. She spoke with strength. She took the lead. She who had been afraid now confidently comforted us in our distress.[5]

A Heroic Homecoming

When I first met Dayna and Heather, their 102 days of imprisonment had only just recently come to an end in a Hollywood-style rescue from Afghanistan. Kabul had fallen to the Northern Alliance and they were on the run. In a dramatic nighttime rendezvous with U.S. Special Forces, Heather miraculously found matches and burned her headscarf to get the attention of the helicopter searching for them in the dark outside the city. They were transported by military helicopter to Pakistan and flown to Islamabad. What a reunion! Heather was greeted by her father and Dayna by her mother.

These two brave women spoke with President Bush shortly after their release and then began a whirlwind media tour. During a press conference after their release, President Bush commented that it was encouraging just talking with them:

Heather Mercer and Dayna Curry decided to go to help people who needed help. Their faith led them to Afghanistan. One woman who knows them best put it this way: They had a calling to serve the poorest of the poor, and Afghanistan is where that calling took them.... I talked to them right after their release...and I sensed no bitterness in their voices, no fatigue, just joy. It was an uplifting experience for me to talk to these courageous souls.[6]

The girls concluded that first frantic ten days back in the States with an appearance on *The 700 Club.* As a cohost of *The 700 Club,* I had the privilege of interviewing them. While we sat on the set and talked, I was amazed at how humble, compassionate, and articulate Heather and Dayna were as they talked about their faith and the incredible ordeal they had been through. They explained that they knew in their hearts that the prayers of Christians around the world had paved the way for them to be brought home safely.

They knew in their hearts that the prayers of Christians around the world had paved the way for them to be brought home safely.

I had just finished writing my first book, *For Such a Time as This.* As I listened to them explain what had strengthened and encouraged them over the weeks and months before their providential rescue, I thought, *These women are modern-day Esthers!* Curious to know more about them, I took the opportunity to talk with them further after the show. I had assumed that two such courageous and self-sacrificing women must surely have been missionary kids raised in Christian homes. That would explain their radical motivation to travel to such a hostile country and put their lives in danger to share the love of Jesus. To my amazement, I learned that just a few years earlier, these two girls probably would have been considered the unlikeliest of Esthers.

Lest you think this dramatic story is too spectacular—that nothing like this could ever happen in your ordinary life or that you've made too many mistakes for God to ever use you in a powerful way—wait till you hear *the story behind the story.* In fact, this is the part I've been dying to get to, because it encourages me the most.

UNLIKELY ESTHERS

I call Heather and Dayna "unlikely Esthers" because neither of them became set apart for the Lord until their late teens. God took two ordinary girls with no direction and really messy lives and radically transformed them through the love of Jesus Christ.

As children, Heather and Dayna both experienced the pain of divorce. By the time they were in their teens, the consequences of broken homes and lives without the hope of God had taken a toll.

Heather's Story Behind the Story

Heather explained, "I definitely didn't grow up in a picture-perfect home." She remembers a fairly normal childhood, but as she got older her family really began to fall apart. When she was thirteen, her parents separated; they divorced only two years later. Heather and her siblings were split up, and as the oldest child, she felt a responsibility to hold things together. As is so typical in broken homes, the stress took its toll on the kids. Heather and her sister both struggled with depression. To complicate matters, their father had a drinking problem, which added another stressful dynamic to the situation.

That's such a critical age for a young woman, and Heather became very insecure. "There just wasn't any stable place in life," she said, "so for a time I rebelled. I thought, *If my parents are going to do their own thing, then I'll just do my own thing too.*" In order to survive emotionally she got very tough on the outside, but on the inside she was hurting and broken, frail and weak.

For a time, when things got really crazy, she developed an eating disorder. "My life was out of control, but at least I could control this one thing, what I ate or didn't eat. I was angry. I just wanted life not to be so hard. I was depressed and just wanted to cry all the time because everything was so crazy. I had to grow up really fast and I just wasn't ready for it."

I could really identify as I listened to Heather. I too had experienced the instability and insecurity brought on by my parents' divorce. Even the anger and feelings of lack of control, which manifested themselves in an eating disorder, were all too familiar to me.

So how did God interrupt this chaos and transform Heather's life? She beamed as she told me, "Jesus delights in taking the messed-up, broken pieces of our lives, the weak things, the foolish things, and building them together to be something beautiful.

"Jesus delights in taking the messed-up, broken pieces of our lives, the weak things, the foolish things, and building them together to be something beautiful."

"It was God's mercy that gave me a Christian friend in high school," she said, "really the first follower of Christ I'd known." She saw in this girl the kind of love and life she longed for. This new friend came from a Christian home and just had this joy and peace about her. Heather thought, *How does her life look like that when mine looks like a mess?* This girl reached out to Heather and invited her to church.

Heather knew about Jesus, but she had never heard that Jesus loved *her* and had a plan for *her life.* Heather had always had a sense that she wanted to live for something bigger than herself, but she didn't know what that *bigger* was. On that night at church, she found what she had been looking for. Joining hundreds of other young people, she asked Jesus to give His love to her. After the service, Heather went to talk to the man who had delivered the message and led them in the prayer of salvation. When she broke down in tears halfway through her first sentence, the man explained to her that she had received a new life and that Jesus was healing her heart.

Everything began to change. Though Heather's family was still broken, her heart was not. Her outlook on life began to change. Where once there had been pain and insecurity she now found joy and purpose. As Jesus became the center of her life, she noticed that her attitude changed and that her desires and goals were changing too. She also began to notice people who were carrying the same pain she had carried before she heard the message of Jesus' love for her.[7] At first, she shared her newly discovered faith only with people she knew. Then in 1995, when she began attending Baylor College in Waco, Texas, she got involved with a campus ministry to college students and led Bible studies and small fellowship groups.

Heather wanted to be close to people with critical needs and help them without seeming like she was looking down on them, so she began hanging out with homeless people on Waco's street corners and under the interstate bridge. At one point, she even tried to rent an apartment in an inner-city low-income housing project so she could find out what the poorest people in the city really needed.[8] Soon she began dreaming of serving the poor overseas and expressing the love of Jesus to those who had never heard of Him.

One day, as she was wondering if she really had the talent or skill to make a difference in a country as devastated as Afghanistan, God seemed to answer her with three short questions of His own:

- Can you love your neighbor?
- Can you serve the poor?
- Can you weep as I weep for poor and broken people?

Her answer to each of these questions was "Yes, Lord."

Dayna's Story Behind the Story

Dayna's story is just as amazing and inspiring. Dayna's parents divorced when she was just ten. Her mom worked a lot and Dayna often felt like she didn't have a family or any roots to hang onto, so her friends became her family.

By the time she got to high school, she was a party girl, smoking and drinking with her friends. "All my friends were drinking and involved in wrong relationships with guys. I didn't even know it was possible to live a pure life. My morals were all messed up," she remembers. When it seemed like she was the only virgin left among her friends, she finally gave in to the guy she was dating. "I totally thought you could sleep with someone you're in love with and that's fine. But I felt dirty afterward. I felt shame. It wasn't fulfilling at all."

At one point, though, she really committed to waiting until marriage. Then one night she had a date that went very wrong. "We got really drunk and it ended up like a date rape situation. I just remember crying." After that she gave up even trying to be pure. On her seventeenth birthday her actions caught up with her—Dayna got pregnant.

She was terrified of bringing shame on her family, especially her father. "In my twisted way of thinking, I believed that if I had an abortion, no one else would get hurt—just me." I thought, *Well, Lord, send me to hell and send my baby to heaven*. But it wasn't that easy. After the abortion she became rock hard inside—her emotions had become completely dulled. Her life was out of control, and she continued to bury her pain in promiscuity and alcohol.

Dayna was shocked when her aunt found out about everything and told her father. This was her greatest fear; she was sure he would disown her. To her amazement, he just looked at her with tears in his eyes and told her that he loved her. "I couldn't remember him ever telling me that before." The revelation of her father's love—and the realization that her mother wanted to be there for her—is what God used to begin the process of healing.

Even after Dayna's secret was revealed to her family, for a while she continued to party. But when her mom suggested that she go away to a Christian college, she was finally ready to get as far away from her past as possible.

That's when her miracle happened.

At school, she met a girl who really loved God and was full of joy and life. This girl was so different from her friends back home. She began inviting Dayna to church and campus ministries. It was at one of these gatherings that Dayna had an encounter with God like never before. "There was something special about the worship. I remember sensing this presence drawing me in." Then, when a couple of people came to pray for her personally, she said, "It was just like a rushing river. Rivers of heat and love just washed over me and all I could do was weep, weep, weep. I thought, *God really does forgive me and love me, even in the midst of my sin.* After being touched like that, I was hooked."

Dayna decided to give herself to the Lord 100 percent—but she realized she had to make some serious changes in her life. No sex. No guys. No drinking. No secular music. Anything that was not pleasing to God had to go. "I started reading the Bible, and it captivated me. For the first time, I felt clean. I was just falling so much in love with God."

She also started looking for ways to get to know and help some of the young girls that hung out at the local youth center. She felt most deeply for the girls who were pregnant, were addicted to drugs and alcohol, or were in any other kind of serious trouble. Dayna wanted to support them in the same way she once needed support.

Dayna's desire to help women increased as she completed her degree in social work at Baylor and devoted herself to a year of intensive discipleship training through a program called the Master's Commission. Then during several short-term missions trips to Mexico,

Guatemala, Siberia, and Uzbekistan, the Lord began to give Dayna a heart for people in other countries, people who had never heard about God's love.

Dayna has suggested some tools for healing from past sins and growing in your faith: "The Father Heart of God," by Floyd McClung Jr.; "Bondage Breaker" by Neil T. Anderson; and "Victory over the Darkness" by Neil T. Anderson.

During her year in Master's Commission, Dayna went through a Youth With A Mission (YWAM) prayer journal and every day prayed for unreached people groups. And every day it seemed that she was praying for another country with millions of Muslims. "The more I prayed for these people, whom I knew little about, the more God started giving me His burden for them. My heart broke for them, especially the women, who had no idea who God is and that He loves them." Then the opportunity to go to Afghanistan came. "It was like an explosion of the heart," Dayna said. At first she was excited, but then she got scared. *God, I'm not qualified. I'm not some kind of evangelist,* she argued. That's when Isaiah 6:8–9 came to mind:

> Then I heard the voice of the Lord saying, "Whom shall I send? And who will go for us?"
> And I said, "Here am I. Send me!"

Dayna so perfectly summed up God's desire to use *anyone* who will work for Him: "The sweetest thing for me personally is when I speak now and women come up to me and say, 'Thank you! Now I know that God can use me too and that there's healing for me.'"

She continued with this call to rise up: "God wants to call our generation to reach outside themselves, to go to these areas of the world that have never been reached. He's looking to our generation and saying, 'Who will go?' Another sovereign thing is that God is raising up really normal girls. He is stirring our generation to go for it."

Two Destinies Intersect

God brought both Heather and Dayna to pivotal points in their lives, when they were forced to get real with God—about their pain, their sin, and their need for Him to completely change their lives. When they did, their hearts were healed and God began to prepare them for His perfect plan for their lives. Heather and Dayna are examples of how God can take the broken pieces of our lives and make something beautiful.

"God is stirring our generation to go for it."

As I explained to Heather and Dayna my passion for encouraging young women through the example of Queen Esther, their faces lit up. Not only do they relate to Esther because of their own "for such a time as this" experience in Afghanistan; they also want to encourage young women, who are in a downward spiral like they were, to realize and grab hold of the fact that God can completely transform their lives into something beautiful and meaningful.

DESTINY CONTINUES

Since their release from captivity, Heather and Dayna have continued to grow as modern-day Esthers. Along with writing a book about their incredible experience in Afghanistan and releasing a CD of the worship songs that helped carry them through their imprisonment, they continue to travel, telling others about their love for the Lord and for His work worldwide. Their story has been told again and again around the world via television, radio, and print media.

All the money earned from the sales of their book, *Prisoners of Hope: The Story of Our Captivity and Freedom in Afghanistan,* and CD, *Prisoners of Hope: Songs of Freedom,* goes to an organization they formed called Hope Afghanistan. Through their prayers and the funds donated to Hope Afghanistan, which are distributed to people and projects that are helping to rebuild the country, Heather and Dayna are still making a difference.

If you've been inspired by the story of these two unlikely Esthers and want to learn more about Dayna and Heather or find out how you can be a part of fulfilling their God-given vision for the Afghan people, visit their website, www.HopeAfghanistan.net.

Or you can contact them at:

The Hope Afghanistan Foundation
PMB 118
1200 Lake Air Drive
Waco, TX 76710
Hope @ HopeAfghanistan.net

chapter seven

Divine Friendships

kellyewing&kerishea

The Bible's Esther was a girl who understood the value of friendship. After Hegai assigned seven maidservants to Esther, she and her maids spent plenty of time together. These women were undoubtedly impressed by the quality of Esther's character—her kindness, wisdom, virtue, and devotion. These young Persian women had grown so close to Esther that when crisis struck, they were willing to pray to the Jewish God and fast for Esther's people.

And God knew that a time was coming when Esther would need friends she could count on. That's why, working through Hegai, He handpicked a circle of companions for Esther that would support her in her time of need.

God *designed* women to be relational. He understands that friendships are just as important to you as they were to Esther. After all, every girl needs a friend to hang with, to confide in, to hold her accountable, just to listen when it feels like her world is falling apart.

Today, God is still in the business of handpicking maiden friends to help every young lady achieve His divine purposes.

Just ask these two women, Kelly and Keri.

A HOLE OF DESPAIR

Relationships have always been hard for Kelly. The problem dates back to her high school years. When she was fifteen, Kelly's brother died. Adding to her grief, her devastated father withdrew emotionally, at a time when Kelly needed him most. Then, when Kelly was eighteen and in one of her first serious relationships, she was raped by her boyfriend.

The loss of her virginity, combined with her family losses, hit Kelly like a steamroller. She found herself drifting from one romantic relationship to another, choosing to date guys who always expected sex. For years she tried to find fulfillment in shallow, sex-based relationships that never seemed to last.

Kelly's relationships with other girls weren't much better. There was no depth, no intimate sharing, no trust. Kelly's "friends" were out to have a good time, nothing more. Something, she realized, was missing.

"There was a despair there. It was like a hole that I could never get out of," Kelly told me. "I couldn't get beyond a surface level of friendship, whether it was a boyfriend or a girlfriend. I had always felt like I was a good communicator, but I never really had a good buddy, a girlfriend I could dig in deep with."

Not coincidentally, Kelly's relationship with God, which went back to her teen years, was distant as well. She believed in Him and had grown up going to church, but had never really trusted Him as Lord of her life.

What Kelly didn't know was that God was preparing her for a friendship that would change everything.

SET APART

Like Kelly, Keri suffered a significant loss at a young age. She and her father were close during her early childhood. When her father died when Keri was just eight years old, the pain was almost unbearable. She found herself thinking, *How am I supposed to make it?*

Keri's pain was compounded by the fact that she no longer felt she could trust God. She didn't see how a good and loving God could take away her father. Unlike Esther, who lost both of her parents, Keri grew spiritually bitter. She also began looking for fulfillment in romantic relationships that never lived up to her hopes and dreams.

Afraid to be alone, Keri reached a point where she simply decided that she wanted to be married. She got engaged even though others counseled that her fiancé wasn't "the one." Finally, the Lord intervened.

"A few months before the wedding date, my fiancé and I got in a little fight," Keri remembers. "It was the first one we ever had, and the last one. He got up, walked out, and never came back. We've talked since, and he still doesn't know why he left, but I know it was the Lord protecting me."

God wanted Keri set apart for something better. She began to see that it was time to put her trust in Him instead of trying to find satisfaction in a series of broken romances. Keri determined to go on a "dating fast"—not to date another man until she met her husband.

The fast lasted nearly four years. But then Keri's resolve began to waver. She felt a spiritual connection with a male friend and allowed the relationship to take a romantic turn. Yet in her heart, Keri knew that this wasn't God's plan either.

A DIVINE CONNECTION

Kelly and Keri's destinies converged one night in Nashville, Tennessee, at a Christmas party neither had planned to attend. Kelly was going to break up with her boyfriend that night and was in no mood to be social. Keri also didn't want to be at the party. Yet when Kelly reluctantly arrived, she recognized Keri's boyfriend and soon was introduced to Keri.

The girls sensed an immediate connection.

"We started talking about what we did, our jobs, and it just kept leading into deeper and deeper discussion," Kelly says. "I was like, 'I am breaking up with my boyfriend tonight. My whole life is going to change.' And she said she was at the same point with her boyfriend. We were asking each other, *What are we going to do?*'"

Kelly did break off her relationship with her boyfriend that night, and with Kelly's support and encouragement, Keri did the same a few weeks later. The girls were at a turning point, and after so many years of searching for a real friend, both realized that God had arranged for them to play a vital new role in each other's lives.

"Being friends with Kelly means so much more than having a good time," Keri says. "We understand each other. A lot of people think that friendship means having somebody to talk to and have fun with and shop with. All those things are important, but I think real friendship is when you can say something that is not so pleasant to hear, say it in love, and have the other person love you enough to take it and pray about it and see that you are not trying to hurt them."

Kelly admits to many struggles with pride in the past. She didn't want to reveal her mistakes or be accountable to the Lord or anyone else for her actions. But her pride melted as she began to get to know Keri.

"There was such a divine connection with us that I didn't have a choice—I had to spill it, get right what was going on in my life, and push toward a deeper spiritual relationship with God," Kelly says. "There were so many deep, dark sins that I had never confessed. But when I met Keri, I said, 'This is easy. Somebody actually loves me and does not care what has happened in my life. I am a different person, a new creation.' There was a lot of healing for both of us."

In a desire to be obedient to God, both girls made a new

commitment: Not only would they not date until God brought their future husbands into their lives, but they wouldn't even kiss a man again until they were standing at the altar on their wedding day. Though some might see it as a radical or even impossible lifestyle change, Kelly and Keri both felt God's call to recapture an Esther-like level of purity: "Be holy, because I am holy" (1 Peter 1:16).

It wasn't easy at first. But as Kelly and Keri sought the Lord and His perfect will, they found strength and encouragement in each other. Prior to meeting Keri, Kelly had always thought that Ecclesiastes 4:9–10, "Two are better than one, because they have a good return for their work: If one falls down, his friend can help him up," was something she wouldn't fully understand until she was married. But as her divinely ordained friendship with Keri deepened, she realized that the support and accountability they each provided for the other was exactly what God's Word described.

The two of them, as friends, really were better than one.

GOING TO WAR

It was six months after the fateful Christmas party. Kelly and Keri had both prayed about their desire to draw closer to and better serve the Lord. God had responded by opening the door to a missions trip to Ecuador.

Both of these young ladies fasted before the trip, praying that they would have a lasting impact on the teen girls they would be working with. As a result, they experienced an "Esther moment" that took their trust in the Lord to another level.

One night, Keri and Kelly were scheduled to speak to a group of five hundred teen girls. They decided to wear camo pants, orange T-shirts, and black war paint under their eyes. They wanted to show that they were ready to "go to war" for the Lord and these girls, because sometimes it seems like living for the Lord amidst the pressures of this culture can be a battle. So they wore battle gear to help make their point.

Despite their determination, Keri was nervous about speaking to such a large crowd. She wanted to be prepared, so she sat down on her bed to write out notes on index cards.

"My pen just would not write," she remembers. "I scribbled around and it still would not write. I thought, *This is stupid, it's a brand-new pen.* I set it aside, grabbed another one, and it wouldn't write. I grabbed two or three more and they wouldn't write. By the time I got to the fifth one I was actually angry; I was slinging it across the room. We had just a few minutes to get our notes together. The bottom line was that the Lord wanted me to share my testimony, because I had never fully done that. I said, 'All right, Lord, I am going to get up there, cold turkey, and shoot straight from the heart. You are going to have to speak through me.'"

And He did. Keri poured out her heart to those girls, laying bare all the wonderful and painful details of her life's journey. And as Kelly listened, she found the Lord speaking to her too. When her turn to address the crowd came, she set aside her carefully prepared notes and opened up her own heart to the girls. The result was a powerful experience for everyone present.

"It was a blessed time," Keri says. "We were up there to show them that God can do an amazing thing. It's not about who you are or what you look like. It's about what He has done in you. We are totally and radically committed to Him and nothing could ever take that away."

FRIENDS FOREVER

Today, Keri and Kelly are still great friends, still holding each other accountable to their commitments and faith, and still seeking God's heart for their spiritual destiny. They are deeply grateful to Him for handpicking a companion that would challenge each of them to dive deeper into the Lord's love and hang on for the journey.

"When God introduced me to Keri, that was the good seed of a relationship I had never had," Kelly says. "This is a relationship that is never going to break because it was divinely placed by the Lord."

"We are having the greatest time being alive, being single for the Lord, and having this opportunity for Him to mold us and make us and prune us," Keri says. "The Lord just keeps showing us things through our friendship."

Many people who don't know Kelly and Keri well assume that they are sisters. In a way, they're right. These modern-day Esthers *are* sisters in the family of God, pushing and encouraging each other to grow into their destinies as daughters of a heavenly Father.

Like Esther, and like Kelly and Keri, do you have a friend you can count on to pray for you and keep your feet to the fire of your faith walk? Is your relationship with this "choice maiden" based on genuine companionship, loyalty, and integrity?

God wants to bless you with a friend who can help you be everything you were meant to be.

If not, take a look around and pray about it. God may already be preparing a handpicked friend just for you. He loves you and wants to bless you with a friend who can help you be everything you were meant to be if only you will love and trust Him. Pray that the Lord will show you just who He has in mind. As you wait for His answer, you may want to work on developing the Esther-like qualities of a godly friend yourself. The time may be coming when God asks *you* to be that kind of friend for someone in need.

Whether you already have a divine friendship in place or not, don't despair. You already have the best friend any person could want. His name is Jesus. As long as you stick close to Him, you'll never be alone.

chapter eight

Prepared for a Life of Destiny

jenniferrothschild

D o the choices we make at a young age really matter? Let's look at how a girl's choices allowed God to prepare her for a life change she never could've predicted.

GIVING GOD THE REINS

Jennifer was nine years old when she became a Christian, but it wasn't until age thirteen that she felt the Lord's call to draw nearer to Him. Her tender and innocent reply was to give all of herself to Him. She didn't know if surrendering to His will would translate into someday becoming a missionary or a pastor's wife or something she couldn't yet imagine, but she determined to trust Him to shape her life in a way that would be the most pleasing and useful to Him. From that point on, Jennifer conducted her life so that it echoed the words Jesus spoke to His heavenly Father when His destiny moment at the cross was just hours away: "I want your will, not mine" (Luke 22:42, NLT).

Although Jennifer knew that the Lord's path for her life would likely be different from the path she might've chosen for herself, she believed that His goodness and love would pave a way for her that would be far superior to what she would have stumbled upon without His guidance. What Jennifer didn't yet realize was that her obedience would keep the door open for Him to prepare her for a crisis.

A Time of Preparation

As a young teenager, Jennifer's new level of abandonment to God resulted in her following His leading to be more dedicated than ever to memorizing Scriptures. Even though she didn't know why she felt such an urgency to do this, she didn't ignore His call for her to discipline herself in Scripture memorization.

Without the prodding of her parents or a teacher, Jennifer worked to memorize two Scriptures a week, which she continued with for an entire year. Little did she know that, as an expression of His love for her, God was giving her a gift that would prove to be irreplaceable.

God was giving her a gift that would prove to be irreplaceable.

God was at work in Jennifer's life in other ways, directing her to read two specific books, one by Corrie ten Boom and the other by Joni Eareckson Tada. As she read about how Corrie responded to being imprisoned with her sister in a Nazi concentration camp and how Joni dealt with becoming paralyzed in a diving accident, Jennifer couldn't have known that her memory of these women's stories would soon guide her during a time of heartache and loss of her own.

Although Jennifer didn't personally know either of these women of faith, in many ways they became like mentors to her. In both of these women, Jennifer saw resolve and resilience, determination and steadfastness—character qualities she wanted to develop in herself.

If you'd like to read about these women who rose up into the call upon their lives as God took them through adversity, read "The Hiding Place" by Corrie ten Boom and "Joni" by Joni Eareckson Tada.

Unlike so many kids, Jennifer grew up with the blessing of strong Christian parents, and she respected and learned from the examples of unshakable faith she saw in them. Many times she saw her parents remain undaunted during crisis. As she watched their actions and listened to what they said during times of adversity, she noted that they never once turned their backs on their faith, questioned God, or crumbled emotionally.

"What's Happening to Me?"

During a time when most eighth-graders are wondering what it will be like to say good-bye to junior high and hello to high school, Jennifer was wondering why she couldn't see the stairs in the stairwell or the numbers on the blackboard.

From the first moment she noticed that her eyes were beginning to change, Jennifer decided to hide the fact that she was having difficulty seeing certain things. One day, like so many times before, Jennifer was at the mall with friends. She went over to the pay phone to make a call, but this time something was different—she couldn't make out the numbers on the dial pad. Shaken by the fact that she couldn't dial the number herself, she asked her friend to do it for her. Her girlfriend dialed the number but made a snide remark first. Jennifer thought, *Oh no! I don't want my friends to know I can't see!*

When Jennifer finally told her mother that she was experiencing some problems with her vision, her mom took her to an eye doctor immediately. But after a while, prescriptions for stronger glasses weren't helping, so the doctor referred her to Bascom Palmer Eye Institute. After several days of testing, doctors met with Jennifer and her parents and delivered some devastating news: Jennifer had retinitis pigmentosa, an eye disease that was slowly eating away her retinas.

There was no cure. There was no way to correct the damage already done. And the worst news of all? At age fifteen, Jennifer was already legally blind, and her retinas would continue to deteriorate until she was totally blind—unable to see anything at all…for the rest of her life.

With this diagnosis, Jennifer was dealt a life sentence unimaginable to most of us. She would no longer be able to see trees blowing in the wind, return a loving look to her parents, watch the changing face of the sky as the sun rises and clouds dance overhead. She would never again ride a bike, go for a walk unassisted, or see the faces of the people she loved or would someday meet.

As the reality of Jennifer's diagnosis became clear, a chilling silence settled over the doctor's office. The drive home was silent too, as Jennifer and her parents tried to sort out what they had just learned. Jennifer describes what was going on in her mind during that forty-five-minute car ride:

My heart was swelling with emotion, and my mind was racing with questions and thoughts. *How will I finish high school? Will I ever go away to college? How will I know what I look like? Will I ever get a date or a boyfriend? Will I ever get married?* I remember feeling my fingertips and wondering how in the world people read Braille.

And then it hit me.

I will never be able to drive a car.

Like most teenagers, I thought that having wheels was just like having wings. I couldn't wait to drive! That was a step toward independence to which nothing else compared. But now it was a rite of passage I would never experience, and I was crushed.[1]

IT IS WELL

As Jennifer wrestled with these questions, she knew that another question—a bigger question—was being asked of her: How would she respond to this crisis?

Jennifer and her parents arrived home. As they walked through the front door, Jennifer could've done so many things: run to her bedroom and cried, called a girlfriend and shared the horrific news, stomped her feet in anger at God. Instead she walked into the living room and sat down at the piano. Jennifer had never been a dedicated piano student and had only practiced as a way of getting out of doing the dinner dishes, but something drew her to the piano that afternoon.

As Jennifer's fingers moved along the keyboard, the song of her heart was released through her fingertips. The melody of an old hymn— "It Is Well with My Soul"—seemed to leap from the piano keys and break through the silence. Although she did not sing the words out loud as her fingers danced across the keyboard, the words rang in her spirit:

When peace like a river attendeth my way
When sorrows like sea billows roll
Whatever my lot, Thou has taught me to say
It is well, it is well with my soul.

How could it be well with the soul of a girl who had just learned that she would soon be totally blind? Amazingly enough, the answer to that question was right in front of her. In the years leading up to this crisis moment, God had been preparing Jennifer. She had chosen to follow the Lord into those places where He could saturate her spirit with His Word and with examples and testimonies of faith. Not knowing at the time that she would one day be unable to read a regular Bible, Jennifer had committed to memorizing Scripture. And the stories of women of faith she had read had provided knowledge and resources she could now draw on. God had filled Jennifer with Scripture and stories and examples that would never fail her. Because of this obedience to preparation, Jennifer could genuinely respond to God with complete trust. So even though it wasn't well with her circumstances, it was well with her soul.

A NEW GIFT

When Jennifer stepped through the front door to her house that afternoon, a gift from God was waiting for her—the gift of being able to play the piano by ear. It was strange; Jennifer had never considered the idea of playing by ear because music simply hadn't been very important to her. But in the stillness of that moment, as she sat at the keyboard overwhelmed with emotion, Jennifer began to draw into the refuge of Christ and wanted to express through music the tenderness of her heart toward Him.

Even though it wasn't well with her circumstances, it was well with her soul.

Jennifer realized that the few songs she had memorized weren't enough, so she began to play a new song, one she never played before. For the very first time ever, she played with her hands what she was feeling in her heart and hearing in her mind. Whether God was giving her a new gift or bringing forth a gift that had been dormant within her, she didn't know. All she knew was that, mysteriously, the gift of musical art was coming alive in her. As her fingers rolled across the keyboard fluidly, dynamically, creatively, God was moving this modern-day Esther into a new position of destiny.

Within a very short time following her visit with the ophthalmologist, Jennifer was completely blind. She finished high school with the help of family and friends, who supported her in numerous ways. She even overcame her fears and went away to college, where she met the man she would one day marry. She is now a mother of two sons, a recording artist, a speaker, and a published author. In her book, *Lessons I Learned in the Dark,* Jennifer tells how she was able to sit down and play that song even though she was in deep sorrow:

> It's been more than twenty years now since I left the eye hospital knowing that I would be totally blind. But even on that day, I believed that just beyond my despair a doorway of promise was about to be opened by the merciful hand of God. It was the promise that no matter what my circumstances, it could be well with my soul. That's why even amid deep sorrow, I could go home, sit down at our old piano, and play "It Is Well."[2]

ASKING THE RIGHT QUESTIONS

Over the years, Jennifer has seen Romans 8:28 at work in her life: "In all things God works for the good of those who love him, who have been called according to his purpose." As she has remained faithful to Him and not allowed bitterness because of her circumstances to overtake her faith, peace, and joy, God has swung the door wide open to use her hardship to encourage many people.

As people seek to understand the why's of their own suffering, they often ask Jennifer if she understands why God has allowed her to suffer with blindness. Jennifer told me that she has found it counterproductive to ask, "God, why did You do this to me?" Because she loves Him and knows that He loves her dearly, Jennifer instead asks, "Why are You allowing this, God? What is it that You want performed in me through this or because of this?"

In much the same way God used Jennifer's parents and the stories of Corrie ten Boom and Joni Eareckson Tada to prepare her to turn to Him and persevere, God is using Jennifer to encourage others. Jennifer says that an intimate relationship with the Lord, rather than the comfort of our circumstance, must be the priority of our lives:

> God desires peace and contentment for all of His children, and I have found that the more I delight in Him, the more that becomes the desire of my own heart. Oh yes, healing would be an extraordinary prize—a treasure—and God may give it to me someday. But I would still ultimately lose if I were physically whole but lacking spiritually. Without peace and contentment, the joy of healing would be fleeting and shallow, but resting contentedly in Him reveals a depth of grace that I can still be reveling in ten million years from now in His presence, in His house.[3]

Jennifer often tries to help people who are suffering understand that God loves us so much that He often delivers us *through* our circumstances rather than *from* them. "Sometimes God delivers us through the thorns instead of from the thorns. Why? So His grace can grow there. So His strength can sustain us there. And so we can learn how to travel in tandem with Him."[4]

Jennifer also pointed out to me that Shadrach, Meshach, and Abednego would have praised God only from a distance if He had delivered them from having to go all the way into the furnace. Instead they experienced something far deeper, far greater, far more intimate, and far more gratifying when He *joined* them in the fire—and walked through it with them.

God often delivers us through our circumstances rather than from them.

Although Jennifer has never seen the faces of her husband or her young sons, they are a constant source of love, joy, encouragement, and support to her. This modern-day Esther brings to us so many lessons she learned in the dark. Her music, message, and life encourage countless others to look for God's presence in the middle of their hardships rather than withdrawing from Him in bitterness or faith-consuming despair. Like Esther, Jennifer's response to her crisis has become a point of destiny in her life. One of the lessons she has learned best sums up her still-unfolding story:

Until we settle into the position where we've been placed by His grace, we'll never see His strength made perfect there. And we'll never experience the joy of the journey as we follow Him.[5]

chapter nine

Finding Courage in Crisis

Melissa Libby stood at the podium and looked out over a sea of familiar faces. She wasn't used to public speaking, but after recording straight A's all through high school, she had earned the right to address her classmates. The occasion was the baccalaureate service for the Bend, Oregon, high school class of 2003—an exciting night, and typical of graduation events held each June in churches and auditoriums across the country.

But that night, and the days just before and after it, were anything but typical for Melissa. Her world had just been turned upside down.

Only three days earlier, Melissa's mother had died of cancer. Now she was doing more than passing on a few words of advice to her classmates. She was revealing her heart, displaying the brave faith that would carry her through one of the most difficult weeks of her life. Her courage would serve as an incredible inspiration to her fellow students and their families, helping lead at least one of them to commit his life to Christ.

Melissa opened her Bible and in a clear, steady voice read a passage from Scripture:

"Be strong and courageous, because you will lead these people to inherit the land I swore to their forefathers to give them. Be strong and very courageous. Be careful to obey all the law my servant Moses gave you; do not turn from it to the right or to the left, that you may be successful wherever you go…. Do not be terrified; do not be discouraged, for the LORD your God will be with you wherever you go."

JOSHUA 1:6–7, 9

The audience hung on every word. Most of those listening knew about Melissa's loss. Many were blown away that night by her courage, her poise, and what was clearly a deep-rooted trust in the Lord.

Melissa sure wouldn't have asked for the circumstances that led up to that night, yet she recognized that God had given her a rare opportunity to share about her love for Him.

Melissa's faith is a quiet one. She isn't outspoken. She isn't a stand-up-and-take-charge kind of leader. She told me recently that she's "not bold enough to go up to people and say, 'Do you know Jesus Christ?'" Yet in the days after her mom's death, Melissa found herself speaking to large crowds about her Savior—not once, but three times.

At these critical moments, when so many others would have understandably chosen to not even show up, Melissa—just like Queen Esther—found unbelievable courage in the Lord to speak out.

God had prepared this modern-day Esther for a week unlike any she'd had before—*for such a time as this.*

FAMILY MATTERS

Melissa invited Jesus into her heart at the age of six, and from that point on her faith grew steadily. Over the years she spent many hours in her room praying, reading her Bible, and filling up journals with her private thoughts about God and life.

The rest of her family revealed a growing faith too. Melissa's brother was also a believer. Her father worked for a Christian book publisher. And her mother, Laura, taught Sunday school and homeschooled Melissa until she entered high school.

The Libbys were a tight-knit family, but Melissa and her mom were especially close. Melissa loved watching her mother, blond hair shining, eyes snapping with a fire that said, "I love you, my girl." They each had a special place in the other's heart. Sometimes, when both had the same thought at the same time, they would just look at each other and laugh.

A dark cloud descended on the Libby family, however, on the day doctors discovered a cancerous tumor in Laura's gall bladder. Her gall bladder was removed and doctors began a series of chemotherapy treatments. Finally, after a year of chemo and blood tests—during Melissa's junior year of high school—the cancer went into remission.

The Libbys had little time to enjoy the victory, however. Only a few months later, tests showed that the cancer was back. Laura went through more rounds of chemotherapy, which again seemed to get the disease under control.

In the spring of Melissa's senior year, however, the Libbys received another shock. Inexplicably, Laura's cancer had spread. As the days passed, Laura slipped further and further away. What should have been a time of celebration and joy—Melissa had been invited to speak at baccalaureate and as a valedictorian at commencement—instead turned into a period of deepening sorrow.

Like Esther, Melissa never would have imagined the situation she found herself in. But also like Esther, Melissa found strength in the Lord. It allowed her, in her grief, to pour out her love to her mom.

"I felt like I was losing my heart," she said later. "The one who made me feel special was leaving.

"I had to give it all to her. I kissed her more times than I can remember. I got down on her level, cocked my head to look underneath her half-closed eyes, and we'd make eye contact. She couldn't talk, but through her eyes I'd see that place that belonged to just the two of us. I'd whisper 'I love you' once again, in case she hadn't heard it all the other times."

And then, sooner than anyone anticipated, Melissa's beloved mother was gone. The woman who had put everything into raising Melissa and her brother, who had introduced them to the Lord and prayed for them since they were born, was now in His presence for eternity.

Would she speak at baccalaureate and address her class at graduation as valedictorian?

The date was Thursday, May 30. It was three days before baccalaureate. In the midst of this time of incredible loss and sadness, Melissa had to make a decision: Would she speak at baccalaureate and address her class at graduation as valedictorian?

No Coincidence

Looking back on her life, and especially the last year, Melissa realized that God had been positioning her for this moment. In her growing faith and desire to be obedient to the Lord, she had been praying for new, non-Christian friends that she might be an example to. Melissa says that God answered those prayers during her senior year, bringing a whole new group of girls and guys into her life.

One of those friends, a guy named Eric, accompanied Melissa and other members of their church youth group on a week-long mission trip to Mexico earlier in the year. Through the example of Melissa and her Christian friends, God was working in Eric's heart. Melissa understood that speaking at baccalaureate was another chance to let God shine through.

"I don't believe in coincidences," Melissa told me later. "I knew that God wanted me to speak, that He didn't want me to shrink back and hide. He was giving me these opportunities and I was going to use them."

Melissa also knew that her mom would have wanted the same thing.

"She had homeschooled me and worked so hard at that and seen me work hard at it," Melissa said. "She helped me through it. So I knew that speaking was something she would want me to do. It was an opportunity I couldn't pass up."

Even with the decision made, Melissa says she couldn't have done it without feeling God's love through prayer and through the support of her church. Like Esther, Melissa leaned on God in her moment of crisis, and the Lord came through in a big way.

DESTINY MOMENTS

The baccalaureate service itself was an emotional evening. By the time Melissa finished her remarks, encouraging her friends and classmates to find courage in the Lord, there were few dry eyes in the audience.

The person affected most of all, however, was Melissa's friend Eric. During the service that night, right there in the church, Eric quietly invited Christ into his heart. Melissa's testimony had made a difference—one with eternal impact.

Yet even after Eric accepted Jesus, God had more work to do through Melissa. Just two days later, that same church hosted a memorial service for Laura Libby. Eric was there again, feeling scared and unsure. He wasn't yet convinced that his new faith was real.

Melissa's dad, knowing how Melissa and her brother were the center of Laura's life in so many ways, asked if there was any way they could

With a remarkably calm presence, Melissa delivered a moving tribute to her mother that morning.

share at the service. Once again, Melissa sensed a "destiny moment"—that God was behind her father's request, creating a divine opportunity.

Melissa prayed about it, wrote down her thoughts about her mom, and then prayed that she would be able to read them without breaking down.

She did. With a remarkably calm presence, Melissa delivered a moving tribute to her mother that morning. She related a few simple, favorite memories—"the way she wrote my name, kisses, her fresh clean smile, notes in my lunches"—and put together a fitting description of her mom: "Everything about her was clean and perfect and right."

Then Melissa closed with a heartfelt Scripture reading of hope and praise:

> For as high as the heavens are above the earth, so great is his love for those who fear him.... Praise the LORD, you his angels, you mighty ones who do his bidding, who obey his word. Praise the LORD, all his heavenly hosts, you his servants who do his will. Praise the LORD, all his works everywhere in his dominion. Praise the LORD, O my soul.
>
> PSALM 103:11, 20–22

I have no doubt that every person in the church that day was inspired and encouraged by the strength and witness of Melissa Libby. The impact on Eric was life-changing. During the service, he began crying. God had spoken to him, showing Eric that Jesus *was* real and in his heart. He had used a courageous young woman to bring another soul to His kingdom.

No Holding Back

God still wasn't through with Melissa. Graduation was three days away, and Melissa again felt the Lord guiding her to publicly honor not only the memory of her mom, but also the gracious God her mom had served so well while living and who Melissa continued to serve, love, and obey.

During the days leading up to Esther's devastating accusations against Haman before King Xerxes, she certainly had opportunities to back away from the dangerous path she'd started down. Even after she'd made her unbidden visit to the king's courts, Esther could have hosted a couple of sumptuous feasts and left the matter alone. The king and Haman would have been impressed with Esther's serving attitude (and maybe her cooking skills), and neither would've suspected anything more.

But God would have known. Esther knew what God wanted her to do, that He had been preparing her for this moment. It wasn't going to be easy, but Esther made up her mind that she would obey the Lord's will for her.

And so, hundreds of years later, did Melissa.

Almost before Melissa knew it, Friday night arrived. More than three thousand people gathered for the graduation ceremony, which was being held at the local fairgrounds auditorium to accommodate the large crowd. The band played "Pomp and Circumstance" as graduates in blue caps and gowns filed in. Melissa and the other speakers took their seats on the stage.

A student officer welcomed the crowd. The choir sang. A few of the other valedictorians made their own remarks. Finally, it was Melissa's turn to speak.

She rose from her seat and stepped to the podium. Most of the audience knew what she had been through that week. Many were amazed that she was even there. A dramatic hush fell upon the crowded auditorium.

Melissa spoke in a clear voice: "Wow, I can't believe we're finally done. It seems like it went so fast. I want to thank all the teachers here. Thank you for the inspiration you have been and how much you have helped. But there is one teacher who isn't here tonight. She passed away a week ago. I want to thank my mom, Laura Libby, who taught me for eight years before high school. Without her, I wouldn't be here today...

"Allow me to end by reading the lyrics of a song by Cindy Morgan, 'How Could I Ask for More,' that sums up what I've said. I want you to close your eyes and think of the feeling you get with each phrase in this song. I have come to know this feeling as the voice of my God speaking of how awesome He is, and His love for me. He has never let me down, and most of all, tonight, I want to thank Him for that. He is my strength.

"There's nothing like the warmth
Of a summer afternoon,
Waking to the sunlight
Being cradled by the moon
Catching fireflies at night
Building castles in the sand
Kissing Mama's face goodnight
And holding Daddy's hand

"Thank You, Lord
How could I ask for more...

"So if there's anything I've learned
From this journey I am on

Simple truths will keep you going
   Simple love will keep you strong
'Cause there are questions without answers
   Flames that never die
Heartaches we go through are often blessings in disguise

"So thank You Lord, oh thank You Lord,
   How could I ask for more?"

Melissa Libby was the only speaker to receive a standing ovation that night. Her words—and her Esther-like courage—had again touched the hearts of everyone in attendance.

Melissa isn't sure where God will lead her next. She loves working with kids, especially those who aren't from strong Christian families, and is pursuing a degree in elementary education on a college scholarship. Whatever happens, she knows that she has the courage to follow His will for her life.

"I have just decided that you can't hold back," Melissa says. "When God causes something to happen in your life, you can't go and hide. I want people to know the awesome life that God offers, and the hope, and the joy, and everything He can fill your life with."

God doesn't want you to hold back, either. He offers hope and joy to everyone who makes the choice to boldly follow Him. Sure, you may be afraid sometimes—but faith can overcome fear. Christ will give you courage, and that courage becomes faith in action.

chapter ten

Answering the Call

bethany, kristina, & k.j.

I was captivated as I sat on the set of *The 700 Club* and watched TV footage of a young woman praying in front of hundreds of thousands of people in Washington D.C. *Who is she?* I wondered. This brown-haired, freckle-faced young woman had a wholesome, girl-next-door look—yet she prayed with an urgent, almost desperate passion. On behalf of her generation, she voiced a prayer that had been banned in schools before she was even born. She prayed for God to turn the hearts of her generation and our nation back to Him. As she cried out to God, I thought, *I've got to find out who she is. There's something special about her and the other girls and guys who are fasting and praying there.*

I talked to our producer, who put me in contact with one of the coordinators of the D.C. event. As soon as I described this young woman and her passionate prayers, he said with certainty, "Oh, that's Kristina Lotze. She's a remarkable girl."

That's how I first became acquainted with Kristina, the youth movement known as The Call, and a group of young ladies who are completely sold out to living as modern-day Esthers. I have since attended The Call rallies across the country and have seen thousands of young people gather to pray and intercede for others. Over and over, I've been amazed to watch these kids cry out for the power of God. Like Esther, they're speaking out as advocates for a generation and for a nation.

Like Esther, they're speaking out as advocates for a generation and for a nation.

Since that first fall 2000 gathering in Washington D.C., attended by an estimated four hundred thousand people, The Call has put on events around the world: New York City, Los Angeles, Kansas City, England, the Philippines, Brazil, South Korea, and more. As I've watched this groundswell gather momentum, I've become convinced that God is setting in motion an exciting new movement. He is preparing young people just like you for a purpose bigger than anything you could imagine. He wants your generation to make a difference that will rock the world.

It's happening through massive grassroots efforts, it's happening in churches, it's happening in schools, and it's happening in families, one person at a time. More and more of today's youth are responding to God's call to transform our decadent way of life and bring about spiritual revival through prayer, fasting, repentance, and worship.

All those years ago, when Esther realized that she had been prepared specifically "for such a time as this," she had the courage to stand in the gap for her people and fulfill God's purpose for her life. Today, I am seeing more and more young women with that same courage and passion for the Lord and for the people of their generation—girls who, like Esther, are making the radical choice to pray, to fast, and to be set apart for God.

Let's meet three of them.

Standing Up and Speaking Out

At age seventeen, Kristina Lotze felt that God had a purpose in mind for her life. She just didn't know what that purpose was.

A dedicated student, she had been homeschooled and completed her junior and senior years of high school in one year. As she pondered her future, Kristina thought of a number of role models in her life who had all attended an intensive, twelve-month discipleship program called Master's Commission. She decided to work and save money during what would have been her senior year so she could enter the program.

At Master's Commission, Kristina began delving into the story of Esther. She identified with Esther in more ways than one. Kristina's biological father had abandoned her family about the time she was born, yet Kristina enjoyed a wonderful "Mordecai relationship" with her adoptive dad. She also connected with the fact that Esther, though still a teenager, was willing to step off the safe, conventional path and speak up for others.

Through many conversations during her childhood, Kristina's dad had already planted in her heart a desire to continue the godly destiny started by previous generations—to be the next link in God's plan. God was about to take Kristina's desire, combine it with her willingness to speak out, and create a divine opportunity. Kristina still remembers the moment in her Spokane, Washington, home when she first learned about a prayer gathering being planned for the nation's capital.

"I was sitting at my kitchen table when I heard about it, and I just couldn't stop crying," she says. "I was like, 'I have to go. I have to be there.' That was an ultimate dream come true for me, to be with my generation crying out to God for our nation. How much better can it get?"

Knowing the power of prayer and fasting—and remembering

Esther's decision to pray and fast for three days before approaching King Xerxes—Kristina made her own commitment to pray and fast for God's favor on The Call. It was a rewarding time.

"I had never fasted so much in my life," she told me. "I found out I could hear God's voice with so much clarity. It pushed out all the other distractions and things that were competing for my attention. I felt like it set up my heart to focus and hear God."

Near the end of 1999, when she learned that her parents would be traveling to a church conference in Washington D.C., Kristina heard God telling her to go with them. She did, and found herself meeting Pastor Lou Engle, one of the organizers of The Call. In April, Kristina participated in a series of youth rallies and prayer gatherings for The Call hosted by Pastor Engle in Spokane. Kristina became even more excited about the upcoming D.C. event. Yet even as she and others prayed for the rally that fall, God was preparing Kristina for an "Esther moment."

Only a few months earlier, Kristina wouldn't have even imagined the possibility of standing on a stage in the nation's capital, praying from her heart in front of thousands of people and a national television audience. "I could hardly get up and share my personal testimony without having an emotional breakdown," she says. "I was scared to speak in front of people. I was so afraid of what people would think of me."

God, however, was preparing Kristina's heart.

Not long after the Spokane rallies, Kristina's parents received a phone call. It was Lou Engle. He and his wife felt that God had spoken to them, directing them to ask Kristina to speak at The Call. Before she knew it, this sweet, unassuming twenty-year-old from the Northwest was in the spotlight, pleading with God to forgive a nation's broken covenants, urging a generation to choose "a cause and purpose beyond ourselves," and boldly delivering a prayer that the government had banned from public schools in 1962:

"Almighty God, we acknowledge our dependence on You and beg Your mercy on us, our parents, our teachers, and our nation."

It was an incredible time, and a snapshot of what God has in mind for Kristina's future. Today, at twenty-three, Kristina is in another period of preparation. She expects to pursue a degree in international and political studies and hopes to use her education to bring biblical principles to tomorrow's political, economic, and social systems.

Kristina also leads a group of younger girls in her church and is mentoring those who are coming up behind her to answer the Call. And she has become a great encouragement to me in my writing and in sharing the message of Esther with this generation of young women. She is a quiet warrior for the cause, and I am grateful.

This is one young lady who, like Esther, has her eyes focused on much more than herself and her problems.

"I would really encourage young women to have long-term vision."

"I would really encourage young women to have long-term vision," Kristina says. "Don't just think about today; think about five years from now, ten years from now, twenty years from now, keep thinking into the future. Where do you want to be? Who has God created you to be? How are you going to become that person?

"Esther served the purpose of God, for her generation and for an entire nation. That is a constant encouragement to me. I want to be someone who serves the purpose of God in my generation."

SET APART EACH DAY

It seems as if Bethany Yeo has always felt spiritually set apart. Even as a little girl she had a strong desire to seek God. She remembers that after her parents prayed for her at night, tucked her into bed, and left the room, she would crawl out again to pray on her knees, telling God that she wanted to be with Him and hear His voice.

Bethany was in just fourth or fifth grade when she began to realize God's purpose for her life. She was watching a Teen Mania video, listening to a song about taking the fire of God to the world, when she felt Him speaking to her.

"I felt it in my spirit," Bethany told me. "I was like, 'What is this?' I remember it just made me want to pray. I suddenly *knew* that I really had a passion for missions and evangelism."

In the years that followed, Bethany's passion for taking God to the world continued to grow. At the age of twenty-one she was working alongside her mother, Marlene, who is associate pastor of Grace Ministries International in Brentwood, New Hampshire. Bethany was at a conference when she heard people talking about the idea of a massive gathering of youth at the nation's capital.

"My heart just leapt," Bethany says. "I said, 'Lord, this is the answer to my prayers.' I had already dedicated my Friday and Saturday nights to praying and fasting and believing that God would raise up a grassroots movement for our generation, and now this was going to be the fulfillment of that."

Bethany decided to go all out in seeking God's favor. She committed to a forty-day fast in order to pray for the event that became The Call. She also stayed in touch with other involved friends. Eventually, Bethany and her mother became The Call's New Hampshire coordinators, sending out mailings and communicating with rally organizers.

At a New Hampshire gathering on behalf of The Call, Bethany, like Kristina, met Lou Engle. But it was when Bethany began praying at the event that she really captured the pastor's attention.

Bethany hadn't even planned to speak. But when Lou began

praying for the crowd to come out of their "caves of insecurity" and surrender to God's will, Bethany realized that she had to step to the microphone. The words of her prayer rang with eloquence and urgency as she cried out for God's glory to cover her generation.

"Lou actually turned around—he was quite a ways in front of me—and started charging at me," Bethany says. "He grabbed me and said, 'I need you to pray at The Call! We need the fire in the spirit that you have.' It was just amazing how God orchestrated that whole thing. Now Lou's become very much a spiritual father to me."

That September, Bethany joined Kristina and so many others on a platform in Washington D.C. She prayed that her generation would feel God's relentless love, that they would be brought forth in purity, and that they would be wholeheartedly devoted to Him.

I experienced firsthand the fire with which Bethany prays. I had been asked to come speak at a leadership conference called The Nazarite Gathering, made up mostly of young people who had come together at The Call. I had heard of this girl with a message of holiness who prayed with passion like Kristina but had never met her.

If you'd like more information on The Call, check out www.thecall.com.

After I spoke on the message of Esther (my favorite!) and challenged the girls and guys to live passionate lives set apart for a holy purpose, kids began pouring to the front of the sanctuary, falling on their knees in repentance, and crying out to carry the banner of Esther in this generation. All of us realized that something powerful was being imparted to these kids. I asked Lou Engle and Che Ahn for a modern-day Esther who could stand in and pray with me. Again, Lou charged over to Bethany, grabbed her by the hand, and pulled her onto the platform. I stood amazed as she began to weep and repent for the sins of her generation and call out to God for purity, power, and purpose. I remember thinking that my generation didn't seem to have this kind of passion for God at that age and that I was witnessing a God-inspired thing.

I saw Bethany pray again at The Call N.Y. in 2002, as thousands of young people from the East Coast converged in a park outside Manhattan. Again they came to worship God and pray for revival in New York City, where so much of what directs our culture comes from.

Bethany has continued to show an Esther-like obedience to God and His direction for her life. She still works with her mother at Grace Ministries International and has prayed at a number of The Call rallies. She is active in the International House of Prayer, a nonprofit organization dedicated to establishing twenty-four-hour prayer teams in cities around the world, and Haverhill Outreach Practical Evangelism (HOPE), another nonprofit that meets practical needs and takes the gospel to the homeless.

Bethany has also taken to heart and taught a message right out of Esther. She calls it "A Bride Prepared for a King." Just as Esther went through a purification process as she was being prepared for King Xerxes, Bethany believes that the church today, and in particular her generation, is being prepared as a bride for the Lord, the one true King.

Bethany's message focuses on purity—not only sexual purity, but purity of affection and heart. When she presented it recently to seventy-five girls who were taking a course on the life of Esther, the effect was dramatic. Nearly every girl there rose from her seat and signed a covenant to live fully surrendered to God as a modern-day Esther.

Now Bethany is in a new season of preparation for a future that may include full-time ministry. But whatever path God has in mind, she intends to live her life as an example and advocate for others.

"Even if I never preach in front of multitudes, even if I never have a public ministry, I feel that my life is an act of intercession on behalf of this generation," Bethany says. "I think of my daily choices, choosing to abstain from certain things, even choosing the disciplines of prayer or obedience or worship or meditating on God's Word, as putting another nail in the enemy's coffin. Every time the enemy loses a foothold in my life, I feel like I am gaining a victory for a generation."

"Every time the enemy loses a foothold in my life, I feel like I am gaining a victory for a generation."

GOING TO EXTREMES

Kjirsten Berglund, better known as K. J., was first described to me as a walking "sign and wonder." K. J. says she's always been an "all or nothing" girl—a person who goes to extremes. For much of her childhood, "nothing" would have described how she felt about her life and faith. She moved often and had few friends; she was disillusioned with the church; she was depressed and at times even suicidal.

Then came Valentine's Day 1999, two days before her fourteenth birthday. She was sitting in the back of her church, "totally unengaged," when the worship leader starting singing a song based on Song of Solomon 8:6: "Set me as a seal upon your heart…for love is as strong as death" (NKJV).

Suddenly, everything changed.

"I literally felt something rip out of my heart," K. J. says. "I was on the floor, sitting there bawling, for forty-five minutes. I don't even know how to describe it. That whole root of bitterness—it was gone. I felt the love of Jesus in every fiber of my being."

The Lord had a future in mind for K. J., one very different from the shadowy path she'd traveled so far. Instead of walking in extreme darkness, she was now experiencing the Lord's extreme love. And like Esther, she was about to enter a season of preparation.

Filled with awe over what the Lord had done in her life, K. J. began getting up an hour early each day to spend time with Jesus. Then she decided to go on a forty-day fast, spending three to five hours each day in prayer and intercession for the lost.

Yet K. J.'s dramatic encounters with heaven were not over. At midnight on the night before she was to enter ninth grade in a public high school, K. J. woke up and heard the Lord's voice saying, "Take this year and get to know Me." In obedience, she talked with her parents and withdrew from the public school so that she could spend more time with the Lord. She was homeschooled that year and also worked at the International House of Prayer (IHOP) in Kansas City.

In fact, true to her go-for-it personality, K. J. spent most of every day—and often much of her nights—in the IHOP prayer room, either helping run the child care program, doing her homework, or praying about whatever was on her heart. She also began studying the book of Esther and praying specifically that the Lord would give her a double portion of the spirit of Esther.

K. J. also prayed at The Call N.Y. summer of 2002. It was a sweltering day. That's where I finally met her and interviewed her. The first time I saw her she was facedown on the stage weeping in intercession. I had already arranged to connect with her there based on what I had heard about her. As I asked around, someone said, "You're looking for K. J.? That's her on stage."

Today, K. J. is still working at the House of Prayer, where at age eighteen she is the youngest full-time intercessor on staff. She continues her radical commitment to fasting and praying on behalf of her generation.

"I'm fasting because I have a lovesick heart," she says. "I want to see a generation that won't be afraid to pray in their schools. I want to see a spirit of intercession, which is the spirit of Esther, released on this generation, because we know that when we pray, God moves.

"You see hopelessness in so many people's eyes. We're dead to the Spirit because of television, immorality, all sorts of things. But God is raising up forerunners who will face this generation and be a burning and shining light in the midst of darkness. I want to see a generation set free."

THE CALL CONTINUES

Recently, at The Call L.A. in 2003, I got to see the girls again. Everyone knew it was going to be a powerful day of prayer when the L.A. basin was rocked by an earthquake at 4:30 A.M. God had everyone's attention, and He was ready to shake up the pornography capital of the world. Again it was a full day, from dawn to dusk, dedicated to nonstop worship, prayer, and fasting, this time at the Rose Bowl in Pasadena. I had been asked to pray specifically for revival in the media and for the calling of Esther to fall on this generation.

By now I was well acquainted with these and other young women I regard as modern-day Esthers who have come forth through The Call movement. Initially I had admired these young women for their radical faith and desire to make a difference for God in this world, and now I couldn't help but feel a little bit like a big sister to them. Talking with them throughout the day, I was once again impressed by their maturity, knowledge of the Word, and abandonment to God. It was a touching moment for me as I asked these girls to join me on stage, joining hands and praying in front of thousands for young women to turn from the lies of this world and rise up as modern-day Esthers. The shouts and cheers of affirmation were deafening as a sea of girls and young women across the stadium answered the call.

IT'S TIME TO JOIN!

Now that you've read the stories of Kristina, Bethany, and K. J., I hope you're as excited as I am. These three young ladies are just the tip of the iceberg. Right in the middle of a culture characterized by decadence, immorality, and apathy, God is on the move, preparing a group of girls to go before Him, setting a radical course that will allow His glory to break through.

Esther was a young woman with a heart for God. When the Lord handed her unique opportunities—and unexpected responsibilities—Esther did not turn away from her heavenly Father. Instead, she fasted and prayed, seeking His purposes, and discovered that God had been preparing her for just such a time.

Right in the middle of a culture characterized by decadence, immorality, and apathy, God is on the move.

Esther was already a woman of purity and character. When the divine moment arrived, Esther displayed the qualities that God had planted in her heart: obedience, courage, wisdom. As a result, a people and a nation were saved—and Esther had fulfilled her God-given destiny.

Today, more and more girls are choosing to pursue *their* God-given destiny. Like Kristina, they are finding the courage to speak out and pray for a cause and purpose beyond themselves. Like Bethany, they are making godly choices each day that are victories and acts of intercession for their generation. Like K. J., they are going all out, committing to an extreme life of fasting and prayer in order to bring hope and light to the world.

God has a plan—a destiny—for you too. He is preparing you for a purpose that only *you* can fulfill. You have a part to play in continuing the efforts of past generations and shaping history. God is calling you to be a modern-day Esther, to live set apart *for such a time as this.*

The girls and young women of Generation Esther are waiting for you. Won't you join them?

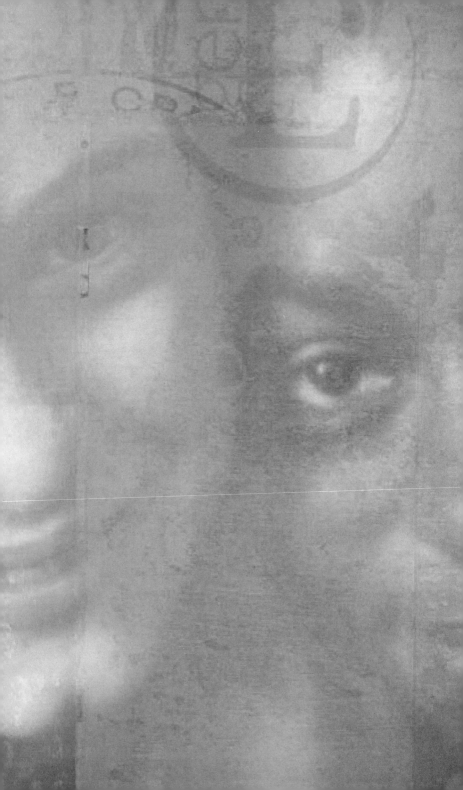

Esther Like You

lisaryan

Seeing what God has done in someone else's life, like the girls you've just read about, can be the inspiration—and the pivotal point—for us to say, "God, if You can do that in her life, what can You do in mine? Do You really have a plan and purpose for my life that I need to be preparing for?"

Forget reality TV. These courageous stories I've shared with you *are* reality and are just a handful of the real-life modern-day Esthers that are living it out every day. I continue to meet remarkable young women with amazing stories—at girl and youth conferences, through e-mail, by reputation, and by divine appointment.

AN ESTHER IN CHINA

Like Huan from China, who e-mailed to tell me about her Esther experience. Though the government in China "allows" people to have their own faith, there is still a very real repression of religion. Huan had become a Christian while attending the university, but found it hard to study her newfound faith in the dorm setting. In China there is a mandatory six people per dorm room, which became so noisy at times that she couldn't study or sleep. The other girls chatted, played cards, and stayed up late.

"I nearly went mad," Huan told me. "Even more, I had no private time to read my Bible, pray, and worship. I desperately wanted private time with the Lord and cried out and asked God for help to leave the dormitory for a while till I grew stronger in my faith. I could hear His words encouraging me that He would take me to a quiet place and set me apart from others."

But this was impossible, she thought. The only rooms available were for postgraduates, and she was still an undergrad. It was also forbidden to live out of the dorms. As a step of faith, Huan inquired about the possibility of a private room and was assured that it was against the rules.

So you can imagine her shock when just two days later the manager of the dorms came to her and told her a private room was available and that she could have it for the rest of the semester. "I was so happy I almost knelt down right there," she said. "The thing that was impossible for humans is a piece of cake for God."

The room was clean and quiet and had a beautiful view of the ocean. The best part was that Huan could freely read her Bible and pray every night. Right around the time when Huan moved into her private room, someone gave her a copy of *For Such a Time as This*. As she devoured the book, she was shocked to find that God had also set Esther apart in her own suite in the palace during her time of preparation. Huan felt like she was God's own Esther in China, and she cherished this special time and place God had given her.

Huan is now strong in her faith and courageously shares her love for God with others on campus in a land still resistant to Christianity.

AN ESTHER ON CAMPUS

Lizi Beth is another story of choices and courage. It was Lizi's first day of high school, and she was overwhelmed. She felt lost in the midst of thousands of students. She didn't have any classes or breaks with anyone she knew from junior high. That day, she went home crying and begged her mom to let her transfer to the much smaller Christian high school in the safe and secure environment of her church. Lizi's mom hesitated because the private school was twenty minutes away and an expense they hadn't budgeted for.

"My mom thought about it for a while, and then, because I have such a great mom, she said yes, as long as I stayed there for all of high school. I was sooo relieved."

The next day they went to enroll Lizi in the Christian school. But strangely, as Lizi walked the halls of the school and was about to get her books, the Lord began to speak to her. "God was telling me that even though this was a great school and all, this wasn't where He wanted me. He wanted me in that big school I hated because He had a plan for me. I just didn't know what it was yet."

Sure, it might be easier to go to the small private school where she knew everybody and there wasn't as much peer pressure, but for some reason God wanted Lizi in that public school, perhaps to be a light in the darkness. Lizi and her mom agreed that if she was still unhappy after a semester she could transfer.

Early that fall, Lizi's church had a youth friend day. So gutsy Lizi got out there and invited a bunch of kids from school, not really expecting anybody to come. "All this time I was still hating school," she said, "and then the coolest thing happened." To Lizi's surprise, eight kids showed up at church

God's got a "Girl Thing" goin' on. The question is, are you part of it?

with her that day. Kids she barely knew. The best part was that one of the girls got saved that day. Most of those same kids and many more are now coming to church with Lizi every week.

"It was just so awesome," Lizi said. "I can't even explain it. There was a reason why God wanted me to stay at that high school. I absolutely love it there now and am bringing more and more kids to church with me."

Through her obedience, God has given Lizi favor and positioned her to boldly and courageously touch her world, her school, and her class with God's love. Just think, where would all those kids be now if she hadn't been there, for such a time as this?

A BRIO BABE

Stephanie Acosta Inks is yet another impressive young lady. I met her at a BABES Seminar in California. Yes, that's BABES—Beautiful, Accepted, Blessed, Eternally Significant. A finalist for *Brio* magazine's Girl of the Year in 1999, Stephanie is a striking Hispanic girl whose composure and maturity grab your attention right away. Kind of like Esther's quietly confident inner beauty drew people to her. Stephanie and I were both featured speakers for the BABES event. As I watched this articulate twenty-something captivate an audience of her peers with a transparent message of choices, the challenges this generation faces, and living a life of purpose, I thought to myself, *Now there is a modern-day Esther.*

Stephanie came to know the Lord as her Savior when she was five years old. She remembers at age seven working alongside her mother in service organizations and volunteering to help even the poorest of the poor in her community. Observing her mother's gentle and kind way with people gave Stephanie compassion and a burden for the oppressed that she carries to this day. Even at that young age she was aware of God's purpose for her life.

This purpose and passion carried Stephanie through her teens. Not only did she honor the Lord in her academics, which won her a bunch of scholarships when she graduated, but she also set up new volunteer organizations every time her family moved to a new community. When other girls were hanging out at the mall or the movie theater, Stephanie was feeding the poor and loving the fatherless. When Stephanie was thirteen, her mother took in two young children who had been in the care of their grandmother. The children and their grandmother were enveloped by Stephanie's loving family, who take these Scriptures seriously:

> Religion that God our Father accepts as pure and faultless is this: to look after orphans and widows in their distress.
>
> JAMES 1:27

> God sets the lonely in families.
>
> PSALM 68:6

As a surrogate sister, Stephanie knew this was the beginning of her mentoring and becoming an advocate for the fatherless.

Graduating from high school as salutatorian, Stephanie went on to Hillsdale College and Oxford with full scholarships. It was there that the heart of this young advocate really took flight. For the first time, she was away from family and friends. And loneliness began to set in. So, as usual, she looked for a place where she could volunteer and get to know her new community. A nonprofit mentoring program in Hillsdale was about to fold due to lack of interest and funding. Stephanie was asked to take it on and try to breathe some life into it. She was terrified and knew this was too much for her, but was quickly reminded that it wasn't too big for God. Some sage words of advice gave her the courage to take on this noble task: "God doesn't call the equipped, he equips the called."

All she had to do was be obedient.

At just nineteen, Stephanie was the girl for the job—a *volunteer job,* that is. In no time, the One-on-One Mentoring Program went from being a one-woman operation, operating out of her dorm room, to a full-blown office with a staff of ten. Stephanie was now running the organization like a business, raising funds through public speaking and managing a staff. And she has done all this on top of keeping up a 3.7 GPA and teaching Sunday school.

To meet Stephanie, you would immediately notice that she's very humble and gracious, but her energy and passion are also compelling. In fact, her senior thesis was on the "scriptural obligation to care for the fatherless." This has become the mission statement for her life.

Stephanie graduated from college in May 2003, with more accomplishments and credits to her name than any young woman I've ever met. Credits like interning on CNN's *Burden of Proof* and at the United States Department of Labor in Washington D.C. But the thing Stephanie is most proud of is the privilege of being part of a God thing through One-on-One Mentoring.

Stephanie has moved on to the next chapter in her destiny preparation. It's actually a quiet, set-apart time of waiting on God's direction—and it's driving her crazy. Believe me, you have not heard the last of Stephanie Acosta Inks. She is a true modern-day Esther for such a time as this.

AND THE DESTINY CONTINUES...

The list goes on and on. So be encouraged! If you have chosen to live a radical life, abandoned to God's purposes, you aren't alone. You are part of a supernatural movement of young women who one by one are standing up, speaking out, and setting a standard. They're setting a standard in stark contrast to the sexy, selfish-girl image this culture has embraced.

God's got a "Girl Thing" goin' on. The question is, are you part of it?

If you're inspired by the lives you've read about and want to know more about Esther, an ordinary girl in the hands of an extraordinary God, and about how you can become a modern-day Esther, then pick up a copy of *For Such a Time as This* along with the study guide. There's strength in numbers, so join with some friends and do the study together.

If you've already read *FSATAT* and committed to the sisterhood of Gen-E and are walking out your Esther moments like these girls, then:

Generation E—e-mail me
at lisa@generationesther.com

I would love to hear your Esther story and perhaps share it with others on my website: www.generationesther.com. Keep the faith, girls. Rise up and go forth...*for such a time as this.*

Lisa

The publisher and author would love to hear your
comments about this book. *Please contact us at:*
www.multnomah.net/lisaryan

I would also like to dedicate this book to the many girls at Mercy Ministries who are courageously facing crisis in their young lives: unplanned pregnancies, alcohol and drug addiction, emotional and eating disorders. These girls have chosen to face their fears and confront the lies of the enemy. Every day, God is radically redeeming them and exchanging their crisis for lives of destiny and purpose. I have the deepest admiration for their courage.

If you are a girl in crisis, or want to help support a ministry that offers real hope to girls, contact:

Mercy Ministries
P.O. Box 111060
Nashville, TN 37222-1060
1-800-922-9131
(615) 831-6987
www.mercyministries.com

The tithe from this and other books by Lisa Ryan goes to support the sacrificial work of Mercy Ministries, both its founder, Nancy Alcorn, and the staff, for their endless commitment to the belief that God can save girls the world has given up on.

Chapter 2

1. The Alan Guttmacher Institute, "Abortion Incidence," Table 1: Number of Reported Abortions, Abortion Rate and Abortion Ratio, U.S., 1975-1996, www.age-usa.org/pubs/journals/3026398.html (accessed 4 February 2003). The most recent Guttmacher data for actual abortion statistics is from 1996. Thus, the 42 million abortion statistic is based upon available date and an extrapolation of trends for 1997-2002, approximately to be one million abortions per year. This trends analysis was taken from Family News from Dr. James Dobson, January 2003, Focus on the Family, Colorado Springs, CO 80995, Issue 1.

Chapter 3

1. Deanna Broxton, "The Top Five Women in Christian Music," *Christian Music Planet* (September/October 2002), 9.
2. Ibid.
3. Rebecca St. James, *Wait for Me* (Nashville, Tenn.: Thomas Nelson, 2002), xi.
4. Richard Vara, "The Voice for the Abstinence Message," *New York Times News Service* (30 November 2002).
5. Joshua Harris, *Boy Meets Girl* (Sisters, Oreg.: Multnomah Publishers, 2000), 31.
6. St. James, *Wait for Me,* 48.
7. Ibid., 37.
8. Ibid., 38.

Chapter 5

1. Lisa Bevere, *Kissed the Girls and Made Them Cry* (Nashville, Tenn.: Thomas Nelson, 2002), 97.

Chapter 6

1. Dayna Curry and Heather Mercer, *Prisoners of Hope* (New York: Doubleday, 2002) and (Colorado Springs, Colo.: WaterBrook, 2002), 179.
2. Ibid., 214.
3. Ibid., 215.
4. Ibid., 227.
5. Ibid., 259.
6. Ibid., back cover.
7. Ibid., 18.
8. Ibid, 21.

Chapter 8

1. Jennifer Rothschild, *Lessons I Learned in the Dark* (Sisters, Oreg.: Multnomah, 2002), 19.
2. Ibid., 211.
3. Ibid., 202.
4. Ibid., 158.
5. Ibid., 161.

Learn to Be a Princess in God's Court

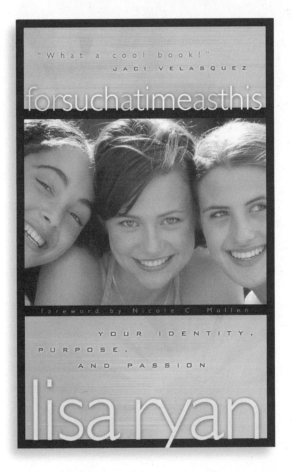

Today's young women are bombarded with messages contrary to the Christian life. They need a clear vision of purpose in order to walk as "princesses in God's court." *For Such a Time as This* by Lisa Ryan, cohost of *The 700 Club*, helps young women find their unique gifts and destinies. It draws on the biblical example of Esther, as well as modern-day role models, to deliver nugget-sized lessons on purity, courage, identity, and destiny. *For Such a Time as This* will transform young readers into mature women of God.

ISBN 1-57673-785-3

YOUR PERSONAL STUDY GUIDE TO FINDING IDENTITY, PURPOSE, AND A PASSION

For Such a Time as This Study Guide

Just as the biblical Esther needed a year of preparations before she became queen, a modern Esther needs preparation to fulfill her destiny. In this in-depth companion study to *For Such a Time as This,* young women follow Esther's example to shape their unique gifts and destinies in a way that will set them apart from the world. Interactive lessons equip them to develop character traits such as courage, purity, obedience, and humility—transforming them into mature women of God.

ISBN 1-59052-174-9